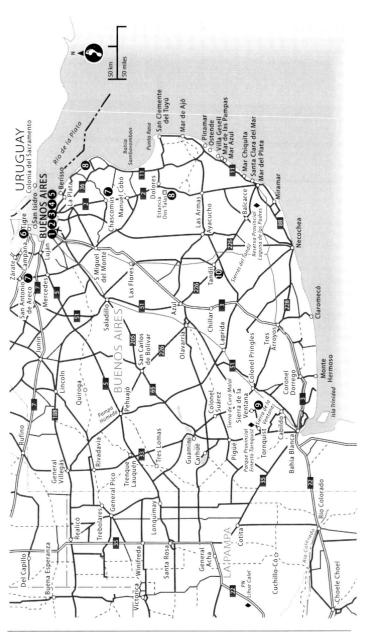

Buenos Aires & The Pampas

Lucy E Cousins

Credits

Footprint credits

Editor: Alan Murphy
Production and layout: Angus Dawson,
Elysia Alim, Danielle Bricker
Maps: Kevin Feeney
Managing Director: Andy Riddle
Commercial Director: Patrick Dawson
Publisher: Alan Murphy
Publishing Managers: Felicity Laughton,
Nicola Gibbs
Digital Editors: Jo Williams, Tom Mellors
Marketing and PR: Liz Harper
Sales: Diane McEntee
Advertising: Renu Sibal
Finance and Administration:
Elizabeth Taylor

Photography credits
Front cover: Shutterstock/Neale Cousland
Back cover: Shutterstock/Neale Cousland

Printed in Great Britain by CPI Antony Rowe,
Chippenham, Wiltshire

MIX
Paper from
responsible sources
FSC www.fsc.org FSC® C013604

Publishing information
Footprint *Focus Buenos Aires & The Pampas*
1st edition
© Footprint Handbooks Ltd
September 2011

ISBN: 978 1 908206 26 8
CIP DATA: A catalogue record for this book
is available from the British Library

® Footprint Handbooks and the Footprint
mark are a registered trademark of Footprint
Handbooks Ltd
Published by Footprint
6 Riverside Court
Lower Bristol Road
Bath BA2 3DZ, UK
T +44 (0)1225 469141
F +44 (0)1225 469461
www.footprinttravelguides.com

The content of Footprint *Focus Buenos Aires &
The Pampas* has been taken directly from
Footprint's *Argentina Handbook*.

Buenos Aires is one of the world's great cities: grand baroque buildings to rival Paris, theatres and cinemas to rival London, and restaurants, shops and bars to rival New York. But the atmosphere is uniquely Argentine, from the steak sizzling on your plate in a crowded *parrilla* to the tango being danced in the romantic *milongas*.

The city seethes with life and history. Once you've marvelled at the grand Casa Rosada (government house) where Perón addressed his people in Plaza de Mayo, and sipped espresso at Borges' old haunt, Café Tortoni, head to the cemetery in swish Recoleta where Evita is buried amid stunning art galleries and buzzing cafés. Take a long stroll around charming Palermo Viejo, with its enticing cobbled streets full of chic bars and little designer shops. Or explore beautifully crumbling San Telmo, the oldest part of the city, for its Sunday antique market where tango dancers passionately entwine among the fading crystal and 1920s tea sets.

Buenos Aires' nightlife is legendary and starts late. You'll have time for your first tango class at a *milonga*, before tucking into *piquant empanadas*, a huge steak and a glass of fine Argentina Malbec at around 2300. Superb restaurants abound; wander around the renovated docks at Puerto Madero, try the trendy eateries of Las Cañitas or the hip hangouts of Palermo Viejo. Or combine the pleasures of fine food and a dazzling tango show.

While there's plenty to keep you entertained in Buenos Aires for a week at least, there are great places to escape to for a day or two within easy striking distance. These include the calm rural *estancies* and the quiet, unspoiled towns of The Pampas, where gaucho culture remains very much alive.

Planning your trip

When to go

Buenos Aires city is wonderful any time of year but is at its best in spring and autumn, when the weather is sunny and mild. The city can be hot and humid in the height of summer, with temperatures over 40°C and humidity at 80%. If you come in summer, consider spending a night in the delta or on an *estancia*, to cool down.

Getting there

Air → *See also page 68.*

Buenos Aires has two airports: **Ezeiza** (officially Ministro Pistarini) ① *T011-5480 6111, www.aa2000.com.ar*, for international flights and domestic flights to El Calafate and Ushuaia in high season, 35 km southwest of the centre; and **Aeroparque Jorge Newberry** ① *T011-4514 1515, www.aa2000.com.ar*, for domestic flights and **Aerolíneas Argentinas** and *puna* flights to Montevideo and Punta del Este, just to the north of Palermo, Avenida Costanera R Obligado.

A display in **Ezeiza** immigration shows choices and prices of transport into the city. The safest way to get between airports, or to get to town from **Ezeiza**, is the efficient bus service run by **Manuel Tienda León** ① *T011-4315 5115, www.tiendaleon.com.ar*, which links Ezeiza with the centre, and hotels (leaving every 30 minutes, charging US$11.50 for the 90-minute journey and US$1 more for transfers to central hotels). They can also organize transfers to Mar del Plata, Santa Fe, La Plata and Rosario. You can pay in pesos, dollars, euros, with credit or debit cards, or book online (return ticket is cheaper). Alternatively, take a reliable Radio Taxi (such as **Pidalo Taxis**, T011-4956 1200), 45 minutes, US$36 – make sure you pay for your taxi inside or just outside the airport at the little booth and wait in the queue. Don't be tempted to just jump in the closest taxis, for security sake. Alternatively you can take a *remise* taxi – these have a fixed fare, and can be booked from a desk at the airport, and charge US$35. There is a local public transport bus which takes between 1½ and two hours and costs US$0.50, but it isn't advisable late at night or early in the morning. **Manuel Tienda León** is the most reliable company, and has a clearly visible desk by Arrivals.

Remise taxi *Remises* charge a fixed fare and are operated by **Transfer Express** and **Manuel Tienda León** (there is a counter at Ezeiza). The journey to the centre from Ezeiza costs US$35 and from Aeroparque, US$6.50. Transfer Express operates on-request *remise* taxis, vans and minibuses from both airports to any point in town and between them.

Taxi Taxis from Ezeiza to the centre charge US$36 (plus US$1.50 toll), but do not have a good reputation for security, and you'll have to bargain. Far better to take a *remise* taxi, see above.

Private transfer Most upmarket hotels will offer a transfer, but you can also organize your own for not much more than a taxi (US$36-40). They will meet your flight, and wait if it's delayed. Recommended is Oscar Carrizo from Remis Executive Transfer, T011-1550 360188 (T+54 911 5036 0188 if calling internationally), o_carrizo@hotmail.com. Contact him with

Don't miss

your arrival/departure flight information, first and last name, number of people, and the address of where you're going to or being picked up from. He only speaks Spanish but is very friendly and very trustworthy.

Aeroparque, the largely domestic airport, is 4 km north of the city centre, right on the riverside, just 15 minutes' drive from anywhere in the centre of town. Manuel Tienda León buses leave every hour from 0900 to 2000 and at 2130, and charge US$4.50 for the 30-minute journey to Retiro, with onward connections to hostels/hotels. *Remises* charge US$6.50 and ordinary taxis US$6. Again, Manuel Tienda León is the most reliable company. Their office in town is near Retiro train station and from here you can order a Radio Taxi. Ask them about their transfer service to hotels in the centre of town. There's a left luggage office here and a phone and banks with ATMs are a block away.

Entry fee

Argentina recently joined Brazil, Chile and Bolivia in charging an 'Entry Request Fee'. Unlike Chile, which charges fees only from the citizens of the USA, Argentina is requesting payment from all citizens of Australia, Canada and the US. Fees for the citizens of above-mentioned countries are:

Australia – US$100, Canada – US$70 (single entry), United States – US$140. Payments are made at the airport and can be made in US dollars, Argentine pesos, by credit cards or traveller's cheque. Although it is not specified, the fees are in theory valid for the life of the passport, except in the case of Canadian citizens who have to pay each time they enter Argentina. **Note** This process has caused queue times to lengthen, so allow more time when booking onward travel.

Prices and discounts

Fares vary considerably from airline to airline, so it's worth checking with an agency for the best deal for when you want to travel. The cheap-seat allocation will sell out quickly in holiday periods. The busiest seasons for travelling to Argentina are 7 December to 15 January, Easter, and 1 July to 10 September, when you should book as far ahead as possible. There might be special offers available from February to May and September to November. Fares usually fall into one month, three month or yearly fare categories, and it's more expensive the longer you want to stay. Return dates must be booked when the ticket is bought, but most airlines will let you change the date for a penalty of around US$100. With student (or under 26) fares, some airlines are flexible on the age limit, others strict, and usually these tickets are the most flexible, though they're not always the cheapest available.

Getting around

Car

It's worth hiring a car if there are several of you, for more freedom to explore the remoter reaches of the country, where buses and tours may not yet have been established. Go carefully though: distances are huge, and road surfaces in rural places are often earth (*tierra*) or gravel (*ripio*), so allow plenty of time – 60 kph is the maximum speed for cars on *ripio*. Apart from the unreliability of the gravel surface, there are unpredictable potholes and rocks in the road, and swerving at speed is inevitably dangerous. Check the vehicle carefully with the hire company for scratches and cracks in the windscreen before you set off, so that you won't be blamed for them on your return. With the exception of roads around Buenos Aires, there's little traffic and roads are single lane in each direction. Service stations for fuel, toilets, water and food are much further apart than in Europe and the United States so always carry water and keep the tank full. Be aware that most Argentines don't use their indicator when they overtake (which they do often), and they use their horn frequently.

Car hire Renting a car costs from US$50 to US$100 a day, depending how big a car you want, and how much mileage (kilometrage) is included: discounts might be offered for longer periods. Busy tourist places are more expensive than quieter towns, but small towns have fewer cars for hire. For most roads, even *ripio*, a conventional car will be fine, but if you're planning to head off into the *puna*, jungle, or remote parts of Patagonia such as the Ruta 40, consider hiring a four-wheel-drive vehicle (4WD). These may be *camionetas* in Argentina – small trucks, high off the ground, and with space at the back, useful for storing luggage and bicycles. Diesel (*gasoil*) cars are much cheaper to run than petrol (*nafta*), although the diesel can sometimes be hard to get. Make sure that insurance is included, and note that the insurance excess (what you'll have to pay if there's an accident) is extremely high in Argentina, because tourists have a history of turning cars over on *ripio* roads.

You'll need a credit card to hire a car, since companies take a print of the card as their guarantee, instead of a deposit. You'll be required to show a drivers' licence (just the plastic bit of a British licence) and minimum age for renting is 25 (private arrangements may be possible). You must ensure that the renting agency gives you ownership papers of the vehicle, which have to be shown at police and military checks, and if you plan to take the car over a border into Chile or Bolivia, for example, you must let the hire company know, as they'll need to arrange special papers for you to show, and the car must have the number plate etched on its windows. The multinational car hire companies (**Hertz, Avis**) are represented all over Argentina, along with Brazilian company **Localiza**, who are very reliable. Local companies may be cheaper, but check the vehicles carefully. Details of car hire companies are given in the Transport sections throughout the book.

Security Car theft has become common in Buenos Aires, much less so in the rest of the country, but park the car in busy well-lit places, where possible throughout the country. Always remove all belongings and leave the empty glove compartment open when the car is unattended to reduce temptation. In tourist areas, street children will offer to guard your car, worth 50 centavos, or outside restaurant areas in cities, there may be a man guarding cars for a peso. It's worth paying, though doesn't guarantee anything.

Colectivo

There is a good network of buses – *colectivos* – covering a very wide radius; frequent, efficient and very fast (hang on tight). The basic fare is US$0.30, or US$0.50 to the suburbs, and you can only pay with coins which you drop into a machine behind the driver. Check that your destination appears on the bus stop, and in the little card in the driver's window, since each number has several routes. Useful guides *Guía T*, US$1.50 and *Lumi*, US$1.80 available at news-stands and *kioskos*, give the routes of all buses. A cheap tour of the city can be had by taking the No 29 bus in La Boca – El Caminito, all the way through to the posh residential suburb of Belgrano (the bus goes further but this trip will have already taken you at least an hour). You will pass by colonial houses in San Telmo, the Casa Rosada, the wonderful buildings of the Tribunales, the bustle of Marcelo T Alvear and Avenida Santa Fe with its nearby shops, trendy Palermo. Take your leave in Belgrano near *Subte* stop Juramento and catch the quick and efficient *Subte* back to the city.

Subte (Metro)

The best way to get around the city, the *Subte* is fast, clean and safe (though late at night it's best to take a taxi). There are six lines, labelled 'A' to 'E', and line 'H'. A, B, D, E and H run under the major avenues linking the outer parts of the city to the centre. The fifth line, 'C', links Plaza Constitución with the Retiro railway station and provides connections with all the other lines. Note that in the centre, three stations – 9 de Julio (Line 'D'), Diagonal Norte (Line 'C') and Carlos Pellegrini (Line 'B') – are linked by pedestrian tunnels. A single fare is US$0.30, payable in pesos only at the ticket booth, or you can buy a *Subte* Card (www.subtecard.com.ar) which can also be used to pay at some shops. If you are only visiting for a few days it isn't worth the hassle; instead buy a card of 10 rides – interchangeable with friends. Trains run Monday to Saturday 0500-2250 and Sunday 0800-2200. Although it is relatively safe, be extra careful at night. Free maps are available from *Subte* stations and the tourist office.

Taxi

Taxis are painted yellow and black, and carry 'Taxi' flags, but for security they should rarely be hailed on the street. Taxis are the notorious weak link in the city's security, and you should always phone a **Radio Taxi**, since you're guaranteed that they're with a registered company; some 'Radio Taxis' you see on the street are false. Call one of the numbers listed on page 70, give your address and a taxi will pick you up in five of 10 minutes. You may need to give a phone number for reference – use your hotel number. Alternatively, ask your hotel before you leave for the day which taxi company they use, as these will be reliable, and then you can always call that company when you're out, giving the hotel name as a reference. Fares are shown in pesos. The meter starts at US$1.20 when the flag goes down; make sure it isn't running when you get in. A fixed rate of US$0.09 for every 200 m or one-minute wait is charged thereafter. A charge is sometimes made for each piece of hand baggage (ask first). Alternatively, *remise* taxis (private cars) charge a fixed rate to anywhere in town, and are very reliable, though can work out more expensive for short journeys. **Remises Vía ①** *T011-4777 8888*, is recommended, particularly from Retiro bus station. *Remise* taxis operate all over the city; they are run from an office, have no meter but charge fixed prices, which can be cheaper than regular taxis. About a 10% tip is expected. For more detailed transport information, see page 68.

Train

The only passenger services are within the area of Gran Buenos Aires, to Tigre with **Tren de la Costa**, T011-47326343, and an efficient service from Buenos Aires Constitución station south through the Pampas to the coast: via Chascomús to Mar del Plata, Necochea and Tandil, run by **Ferrobaires**, T011-43040038.

Tourist information

Tourist offices   The national office ⓘ *Av Santa Fe 883, T011-4312 2232, T011-4312 5550, www.turismo.gov.ar, Mon-Fri 0900-1700*, provides maps and literature covering the whole country. There are kiosks at both **airports** (in the Aerolíneas Argentinas section of the domestic airport T011-4771 0104), daily 0800-2000. There are **city-run tourist kiosks** at ⓘ *Florida 100, junction with Roque Sáenz Peña*; in **Recoleta** ⓘ *Av Quintana 596, junction with Ortiz*; in **Puerto Madero** ⓘ *Dock 4*; in **San Telmo** ⓘ *Defensa 1250*; and at **Retiro bus station** (ground floor). For free tourist information call T0800-555 0016 (Mon-Fri 0900-1700) or for assistance anywhere in the city, call T0800-999 5000 (24 hours).

For city information ⓘ *T011-4313 0187, Mon-Fri 0730-1800, Sat-Sun 1000-1800, www.bue.gov.ar, a great site in Spanish, English and Portuguese*. Free guided tours are usually organized by the city authorities: free leaflet from city-run offices. Audio guided tours in several languages are available for 12 different itineraries by downloading mp3 files and maps from www.bue.gov.ar. **Tango Information Centre** ⓘ *1st floor at Galerías Pacífico, Sarmiento 1551, T011-4373 2823*, is a very helpful, privately run tourist office.

South American Explorers ⓘ *BA Clubhouse, currently moving to a new address, check the website for details or call T011-4307 1309, T011-3475 8200, www.saexplorers.org, baclub@saexplorers.org, Skype SAEBuenosAires, Mon-Fri 0930-1700, Sat-Sun 0930-1300*, offers knowledgeable advice and the clubhouse is a comfortable gathering place for travellers.

Information   Good guides to bus and subway routes are *Guía T*, *Lumi*, *Peuser* and *Filcar* (usually covering the city and Greater Buenos Aires in two separate editions), US$1-9, available at news-stands (*kioskos*). Also handy is Auto Mapa's pocket-size *Plano* of the federal capital, or the more detailed *City Map* covering La Boca to Palermo, both available at news-stands, US$4; otherwise it's easy to get free maps of the city centre from most hotels. *Buenos Aires Day & Night* is a free bi-monthly tourist magazine with useful information and a downtown map available together with similar publications at tourist kiosks and hotels. *Bainsider* (www.bainsidermag.com) is a fantastic resource magazine for getting to know the city (US$1.50 in *kioskos*). Their website is full of useful information. Also free fortnightly online newspaper *Argentina Independent* (www.argentinaindependent.com) in English will be helpful. *La Nación* newspaper has a Sunday tourism section (very informative). On Friday, the youth section of rival newspaper *Clarín* (*Sí*) lists free entertainments. Search Clarín's website (www.clarin.com) for the up-to-date page on entertainment; look at '*Sección Espectáculos*' (in Spanish). *Página 12* has a youth supplement on Thursdays called *NO*. The *Buenos Aires Herald* publishes *Get Out* on Friday, listing entertainment. Information on what's on is available at www.buenosairesherald.com (both newspaper and website are in English). Also see www.whatsupbuenosaires.com for detailed listings (in English) of events, DJs, art exhibitions and basically anything that is going on in the capital. There are countless free publications found in cafés which also have information. There are a few wonderful blogs (in English) as well: www.baires.elsur.org (for an expat's view of the city); www.goodmorningba.com (for forums); www.movingtoargentina.typepad.com (for advice on moving to the city); and www.argentinepost.com (for up-to-date information and news about the country).

Train
The British built a fine network of railways all over the country, which gradually fell into decline through the second half of the 20th century, and were dealt the final blow by handing over control to the provinces in 1994. Few provinces had the resources to run trains and now the few tracks operating run freight trains only.

The only passenger services are within the area of Gran Buenos Aires, to Tigre with **Tren de la Costa**, T011-47326343, and an efficient service from Buenos Aires Constitución station south through the Pampas to the coast: via Chascomús to Mar del Plata, Necochea and Tandil, run by **Ferrobaires**, T011-43040038. There are only two long-distance train lines. One is: from Buenos Aires to Tucumán with **TUFESA**: long, uncomfortable, and not recommended. The other is from Viedma (on the east coast, south of Bahía Blanca) to Bariloche in the Lake District, a more comfortable overnight service which also takes cars. In Viedma, T02920-422130, in Bariloche, T02944-423172, www.trenpatagonico-sa.com.ar. The only other train services are the tourist **Tren a las Nubes**, www.trenalasnubes.com.ar, which runs from Salta up to San Antonio de los Cobres in the *puna*, and the narrow gauge railway from Esquel in Patagonia, **La Trochita** (made famous by Paul Theroux as the *Old Patagonian Express*), http://latrochita.org.ar.

Maps
Several road maps are available, including those of the **ACA** (the most up to date), the **Firestone** road atlas and the **Automapa**, www.automapa.com.ar (regional maps, Michelin-style, high quality). The bigger cities in Argentina have just been added to Google Maps, so this will help with directions, though remember to ask a local as well, to make sure you are heading through an OK part of town.

Topographical maps are issued by the **Instituto Geográfico Militar** ① *Av Cabildo 381, Buenos Aires, T011-45765578 (1 block from Subte Ministro Carranza, Line D, or take bus 152), Mon-Fri 0800-1300, www.igm.gov.ar.* 1:500,000 sheets cost US$3 each; better coverage of 1:100,000 and 1:250,000, but no city plans. For walkers, the *Sendas y Bosques* (Walks and Forests) series are 1:200,000, laminated and easy to read, with good books containing English summaries, www.guiasendasybosques.com.ar, are recommended.

Sleeping

Hotels and guesthouses may display a star rating, but this doesn't necessarily match international standards. Many more expensive hotels charge different prices for *extranjeros* (non-Argentines) in US$, which is unavoidable since a passport is required as proof of residency. If you pay in cash (pesos) you may get a reduction. Room tax (VAT) is 21% and is not always included in the price (ask when you check in). All hotels will store luggage for a day, and most have English-speaking staff. For upmarket chain hotels throughout Argentina contact **N/A Town & Country Hotels**, www.newage-hotels.com. For hostels, see **Hostelling International Argentina** ① *Florida 835, T011-4511-8723,* www.hostels.org.ar, *Mon-Fri 0900-1830*, which offers discounts to card-holders at their 70 hostels throughout Argentina, long-distance buses and backpacker tours. An HI card in Argentina costs US$16. For a complete listing of sleeping options, see www.welcomeargentina.com.

Hotels, hosterías, residenciales and hospedajes

The standard of accommodation in Argentina is generally good, and although prices have risen in the last two years, good hotels are generally very good value for visitors. You'll find that most cities and tourist towns list hotels and *hosterías* as separate: this is no reflection on quality or comfort, but simply on size: a *hostería* has fewer than 20 rooms. Both hotels and *hosterías* will have rooms with private bathrooms (usually showers rather than bath tubs, which you'll find only in the more expensive establishments). Prices often rise in high summer (January to February), at Easter and in July. During public holidays or high season you should always book ahead. A few of the more expensive hotels in Buenos Aires and major tourist centres such as Puerto Madryn, Bariloche and El Calafate charge foreigners higher prices than Argentines, which can be very frustrating, though there's little you can do about it. If you're given a price in US dollars, ask if there's a reduction if you pay in pesos and in cash. Most places now accept credit cards, but check before you come. It's worth booking your first few nights' accommodation before you arrive, and most hotels have an email address on their websites (provided in the Listings sections throughout the book) so that you can make contact before setting off.

Estancias

These are the large farms and cattle ranches found all over the country, many of them now open to tourists, and offering a marvellous insight into Argentine life. Most are extremely comfortable places to stay, and offer wonderful horse riding and other activities such as birdwatching and walking, in addition to the authentic experience of life on the land. They can be pricey but meals, drinks, transfers and activities are included. It will certainly be the most memorable part of your stay.

There's a whole spectrum of *estancias* from a simple dwelling on the edge of a pristine lake in the Patagonian wilderness to a Loire-style chateau in the Pampas. You'll certainly be treated to the traditional *asado*, meat cooked over an open fire, and most impressively, *asado al palo*, where the animal is speared on a cross-shaped stick and roasted to perfection.

Gauchos still work the land on horseback in their traditional outfit of *bombachas* (baggy trousers, comfortable for spending hours on horseback), *trensa* (a wide leather belt with silver clasps), a poncho (in the northwest), a *pañuelo* (neckerchief), a *boina* (beret) and on the feet *alpargatas* (simple cotton shoes).

Estancias can be pricier than hotels, but some are accessible even to travellers on a budget, at least for a day visit. *Día de campo* (day on the farm) is offered by lots of *estancias*, a full day of horse riding, or a ride in a horse-drawn carriage, an *asado* lunch, and then often other farm activities, or time to relax in the peaceful grounds. Overnight stays costs from US$50 for two in the most humble places to US$250 per person for the most luxurious.

Though *estancias* are found throughout rural Argentina, they vary enormously in style and activities. In the province of Buenos Aires you will find *estancias* covering thousands

Sleeping and eating price codes

$$$$ over US$150   **$$$** US$66-150   **$$** US$30-65
$ under US$30
Prices are for a double room in high season, including taxes.

Eating price codes
$$$ over US$12   **$$** US$7-12   **$** under US$7
Prices refer to the cost of a two-course meal for one person, excluding drinks or service charge. Note that most restaurants charge '*cubierto*' which is a cover charge and pays for things like bread and service. These charges can range from between US$1 and US$3 depending on where you are eating and are generally per peson. All charges should be clearly labelled on the bottom of the menu. It is normal to tip about 10% of the meal.

of hectares of flat grassland with large herds of cattle and windpumps to extract water; horse riding will certainly be offered and perhaps cattle-mustering, at La Luisa and Palantelén for example. Some of the finest buildings are in this area, such as Dos Talas and La Porteña. In Patagonia there are giant sheep *estancias* overlooking glaciers, mountains and lakes, such as *estancias* **Maipú, Helsingfors** or **Alma Gaucha**. There are *estancias* on Tierra del Fuego, full of the history of the early pioneers who built them (**Viamonte** and **Harberton**), while on the mainland nearby, **Estancia Monte Dinero** has a colony of Magellanic penguins on its doorstep. There's more wildlife close at hand in the *estancias* on Península Valdés. And in Salta, there are colonial-style *fincas*, whose land includes jungly cloudforest with marvellous horse riding.

The most distinctive or representative *estancias* are mentioned in the text, but for more information see: www.turismo.gov.ar (in English), the national tourist website with all *estancias* listed; www.caminodelgaucho.com.ar, an excellent organization which can arrange stays in the Pampas *estancias*; www.estanciasdesantacruz.com, a helpful agency which arranges *estancia* stays in Santa Cruz and the south, including transport. A useful book *Tursimo en Estancias y Hosterías* is produced by **Tierra Buena**, www.guiatierrabuena.com.ar. You can of course contact *estancias* directly, and reserve, ideally with a couple of weeks' notice.

Cabañas

These are a great option if you have transport and there are at least two of you. They are self-catering cottages, cabins or apartments, usually in rural areas, and often in superb locations, such as the Lake District. They're tremendously popular among Argentine holidaymakers, who tend to travel in large groups of friends, or of several families together, and as a result the best *cabañas* are well-equipped and comfortable. They can be very economical too, especially for groups of four or more, but are feasible even for two, with considerable reductions off-season. If you're travelling by public transport, *cabañas* are generally more difficult to get to, but ask the tourist office if there are any within walking or taxi distance. Throughout the Lake District, *cabañas* are plentiful and competitively priced.

Camping

Organized campsites are referred to in the text immediately after hotel listings for each town. Camping is very popular in Argentina (except in Buenos Aires) and there are many superbly situated sites, most with good services, whether municipal or private. There are many quieter, family orientated places, but if you want a livelier time, look for a campsite (often by the beaches) with younger people, where there's likely to be partying until the small hours. Camping is allowed at the side of major highways and in all national parks (except at Iguazú Falls), but in Patagonia strong winds can make camping very difficult. Wherever you camp, pack your rubbish and put out fires with earth and water. Fires are not allowed in many national parks because of the serious risk of forest fires. It's a good idea to carry insect repellent.

If taking a cooker, the most frequent recommendation is a multi-fuel stove that will burn unleaded petrol or, if that is not available, kerosene or white fuel. Alcohol-burning stoves are reliable but slow and you have to carry a lot of fuel. Fuel can usually be found at chemists/pharmacies. Gas cylinders and bottles are usually exchangeable, but if not can be recharged; specify whether you use butane or propane. Gas canisters are not always available. White gas (*bencina blanca*) is readily available in hardware shops (*ferreterías*).

Eating and drinking

Asado and parrillas

Not for vegetarians! The great classic meal throughout the country is the *asado* – beef or lamb cooked expertly over an open fire. This ritual is far more than a barbecue, and with luck you'll be invited to sample an *asado* at a friend's home or *estancia* to see how it's done traditionally. *Al asador* is the way meat is cooked in the country, with a whole cow splayed out on a cross-shaped stick, stuck into the ground at an angle over the fire beneath. And in the *parrilla* restaurants, found all over Argentina, cuts of meat are grilled over an open fire in much the same way. You can order any cuts from the range as individual meals, but if you order *parrillada* (usually for two or more people), you'll be brought a selection from the following cuts: *achuras* – offal; *chorizos* – sausages including *morcilla* (British black pudding or blood sausage); *tira de asado* – ribs; *vacío* – flank; *bife ancho* – entrecote; *lomito* – sirloin; *bife de chorizo* – rump steak; *bife de lomo* – fillet steak. You can ask for '*cocido*' to have your meat well-done, '*a punto*' for medium, and '*jugoso*' for rare. Typical accompaniments are *papas fritas* (chips), salad and the spicy *chimichurri* sauce made from oil, chilli pepper, salt, garlic and vinegar.

Other typically Argentine meals ➔ *See also menu reader, page 118.*

Other Argentine dishes to try include the *puchero*, a meat stew; *bife a caballo*, steak topped with a fried egg; *choripán*, a roll with a chorizo inside (similar to a hot dog, but better). *Puchero de gallina* is chicken, sausage, maize, potatoes and squash cooked together. *Milanesas*, breaded, boneless chicken or veal, are found everywhere and good value. Good snacks are *lomitos*, a juicy slice of steak in a sandwich; and *tostados*, delicate toasted cheese and tomato sandwiches, often made from the soft crustless *pan de miga*.

Italian influences

It might seem that when Argentines aren't eating meat, they're eating pizza. Italian immigration has left a fine legacy in thin crispy pizzas available from even the humblest pizza joint, adapted to the Argentine palate with some unusual toppings. *Palmitos* are tasty, slightly crunchy hearts of palm, usually tinned, and a popular Argentine delicacy, though they're in short supply and the whole plant has to be sacrificed for one heart. They're often accompanied on a pizza with the truly unspeakable *salsa golf*, a lurid mixture of tomato ketchup and mayonnaise. You'll probably prefer excellent provolone or roquefort cheeses on your pizza – both Argentine and delicious. Fresh pasta is widely available, bought ready to cook from dedicated shops. Raviolis are filled with ricotta, *verduras* (spinach), or *cuatro quesos* (four cheeses), and with a variety of sauces. These are a good option for vegetarians, who need not go hungry in this land of meat. Most restaurants have *pasta casero* – home-made pasta – and sauces without meat, such as *fileto* (tomato sauce) or pesto. *Ñoquis* (gnocchi), potato dumplings normally served with tomato sauce, are cheap and delicious (traditionally eaten on the 29th of the month).

Vegetarian

Vegetables in Argentina are cheap, of excellent quality, many of them organic, and available fresh in *verdulerías* (vegetable shops) all over towns. Look out for *acelga*, a large-leafed chard with a strong flavour, often used to fill pasta, or *tarta de verduras*, vegetable pies, which you can buy everywhere, fresh and very good. Butternut squash, *zapallo*, is used to good effect in *tartas* and in filled pasta. Salads are quite safe to eat in restaurants, and fresh, although not wildly imaginative. Only in remote areas in the northwest of the country should you be wary of salads, since the water here is not reliable. In most large towns there are vegetarian restaurants and, don't forget the wonderful vegetarian *empanadas* such as cheese and onion, spinach or mushroom (see below). Vegetarians must specify: '*No como carne, ni jamón, ni pollo*' ('I don't eat meat, or ham, or chicken') since many Argentines think that vegetarians will eat chicken or ham, and will certainly not take it seriously that you want to avoid all meat products.

Regional specialities

The Argentine speciality *empanadas* are tasty small semicircular pastry pies traditionally filled with meat, but now widely available filled with cheese, *acelga* (chard) or corn. They originate in Salta and Tucumán, where you'll still find the best examples, but can be found all over the country as a starter in a *parrilla*, or ordered by the dozen to be delivered at home with drinks among friends.

Northwest Around Salta and Jujuy you'll find *humitas*, parcels of sweetcorn and onions, steamed in the corn husk, superb, and *tamales*, balls of cornflour filled with beef and onion, and similarly wrapped in corn husk leaves to be steamed. The other speciality of the region is *locro* – a thick stew made of maize, white beans, beef, sausages, pumpkin and herbs. Good fish is served in many areas of the country and along the east coast you'll always be offered *merluza* (hake), *lenguado* (sole), and often salmon as well.

Atlantic coast If you go to Puerto Madryn or the Atlantic coast near Mar del Plata, then seafood is a must: *arroz con mariscos* is similar to paella and absolutely delicious. There will often be *ostras* (oysters) and *centolla* (king crab) on the menu too.

Lake District The *trucha* (trout) is very good and is best served grilled, but as with all Argentine fish you'll be offered a bewildering range of sauces, such as roquefort, which rather drown the flavour. Also try the smoked trout and the wild boar. Berries are very good here in summer, with raspberries and strawberries abundant and flavoursome, particularly around El Bolsón. And in Puehuenia, you must try the pine nuts of the monkey puzzle trees: sacred food to the Mapuche people.

Northeast In the northeast, there are some superb river fish to try: *pacú* is a large, firm fleshed fish with lots of bones, but very tasty. The other great speciality is *surubí*, a kind of catfish, particularly good cooked delicately in banana leaves.

Desserts

Argentines have a sweet tooth, and are passionate about *dulce de leche* – milk and sugar evaporated to a pale, soft caramel, and found on all cakes, pastries, and even for breakfast. If you like this, you'll be delighted by *facturas* and other pastries, stuffed with *dulce de leche*, jams of various kinds, and sweet cream fillings. *Helado* (ice cream) is really excellent in Argentina, and for US$3 in any *heladería*, you'll get two flavours, from a huge range, piled up high on a tiny cone; an unmissable treat. Jauja (El Bolsón) and Persicco (Buenos Aires) are the best makes. Other popular desserts are *dulce de batata*, a hard, dense, sweet potato jam, so thick you can carve it; *dulce de membrillo* (quince preserve); *dulce de zapallo* (pumpkin in syrup). All are eaten with cheese. The most loved of all is *flan*, which is not a flan at all but crème caramel, often served on a pool of caramelized sugar, and *dulce de leche*. Every Argentine loves *alfajores*, soft maize-flour biscuits filled with *dulce de leche* or apricot jam, and then coated with chocolate, especially if they're the Havanna brand. Croissants (*media lunas*) come in two varieties: *de grasa* (savoury, made with beef fat) and *dulce* (sweet and fluffy). These will often be your only breakfast since Argentines are not keen on eating first thing in the morning (maybe because they've only just had dinner!), and only supply the huge buffet-style 'American Breakfast' in international hotels to please tourists.

Drink

The great Argentine drink, which you must try if invited, is *mate*. A kind of green tea made from dried *yerba* leaves, drunk from a cup or seasoned gourd through a silver perforated straw, it is shared by a group of friends or work colleagues as a daily social ritual. The local **beers**, mainly lager-type, are excellent: Quilmes is the best seller, but look out for home-made beers from microbreweries in the lakes, especially around El Bolsón. **Spirits** are relatively cheap, other than those that are imported; there are cheap drinkable Argentine gins and whiskeys. Clericó is a white-wine **sangría** drunk in summer and you'll see lots of Argentine males drink the green liquor *Fernet* with cola. It tastes like medicine but is very popular. It is best not to drink the **tap water**; in the main cities it's safe, but often heavily chlorinated. Never drink tap water in the northwest, where it is notoriously poor. Many Argentines mix soda water with their wine (even red wine) as a refreshing drink.

Wines   Argentine wines are excellent and drinkable throughout the price range, which starts at US$2.50 a bottle. Red grape varieties of Malbe, Merlot, Syrah, Cabernet Sauvignon, and the white Torrontés are particularly recommended; try brands Lurton, Norton, Bianchi, Trapiche or Etchart in any restaurant. Good sparkling wines include the *brut nature* of Navarro Correas, whose Los Arboles Cabernet Sauvignon is an excellent red wine, and Norton's Cosecha Especial.

Eating out

The siesta is observed nearly everywhere but Buenos Aires and some of the larger cities. At around 1700, many people go to a *confitería* for *merienda* – tea, sandwiches and cakes. Restaurants rarely open before 2100 and most people turn up at around 2230, often later. Dinner usually begins at 2200 or 2230; Argentines like to eat out, and usually bring babies and children along, however late it is. If you're invited to someone's house for dinner, don't expect to eat before 2300, so have a few *facturas* at 1700, the Argentine *merienda*, to keep you going.

If you're on a tight budget, ask for the *menú fijo* (set-price menu), usually good value, also try *tenedor libre* restaurants – eat all you want for a fixed price. Markets usually have cheap food. Food in supermarkets is cheap and good quality.

Entertainment

Argentines, of whatever age, are generally extremely sociable and love to party. This means that even small towns have a selection of bars catering for varied tastes, plenty of live music and somewhere to dance, even if they are not the chic clubs you might be used to in Western urban cities. The point of going out here is to meet and chat rather than drink yourself under the table, and alcohol is consumed in moderation. Argentines are amazed at the quantities of alcohol that some tourists put away. If invited to an Argentine house party, a cake or *masitas* (a box of little pastries) will be just as much appreciated as a bottle of wine.

Dancing

Argentines eat dinner at 2300, and then go for a drink at around 2400, so the dancing usually starts at around 0300, and goes on till 0600 or 0700. *Boliches* can mean anything from a bar with dancing, found in most country towns, to a disco on the outskirts, a taxi ride away from the centre. In Buenos Aires, there's a good range of clubs, playing the whole range from tango, salsa, and other Latin American dance music, to electronica. Elsewhere in Argentina nightclubs play a more conventional mixture of North American (lots of 80s classics) and Latin American pop with a bit of Argentine *rock nacional* thrown in, though you'll find a more varied scene in bigger cities like Córdoba, Rosario and Mendoza. **Tango** classes are popular all over the country, and especially in Buenos Aires, where *milongas* are incredibly trendy: a class followed by a few hours of dancing. Even if you're a complete novice, it's worth trying at least one class to get a feel for the steps; being whisked around the floor by an experienced dancer is quite a thrill even if you haven't a clue what to do with your legs.

Music

Live music is everywhere in Argentina, with bands playing Latin American pop or jazz in bars even in small cities. The indigenous music is *folclore*, which varies widely throughout the country. Traditional gaucho music around the Pampas includes *payadores*: witty duels with guitars for two singers, much loved by Argentines, but bewildering if your Spanish is limited to menus and directions. The northwest has the country's most stirring *folclore*, where you should seek out *peñas* to see live bands playing fabulous *zambas* and *chacareras*. The rhythms are infectious, the singing passionate, and Argentine audiences can't resist joining in. Even tourist-oriented *peñas* can be atmospheric, but try to find out where the locals go, like La Casona del Molino in Salta. Most cities have *peñas*, and you'll often see some great bands at the gaucho Day of Tradition festivals (mid-November) throughout Argentina and at local town fiestas.

Essentials A-Z

Accident and emergency
Police T101. **Medical** T107.

If robbed or attacked, call the tourist police, **Comisaría del Turista**, Av Corrientes 436, Buenos Aires, T011-4346 5748 (24 hrs) or T0800-999 5000 (English spoken), turista@policiafederal.gov.ar. Note that you will most likely not get your stolen goods back, but a police report is essential for your insurance claim.

Dress
Argentines of whatever class tend to dress neatly and take care to be clean and tidy so it's much appreciated if you do the same. In the 'interior', particularly outside Buenos Aires, people are more conservative and will tend to judge you by the way you dress. Buying clothing locally can help you to look less like a tourist – clothes are cheap in Argentina in comparison with Western Europe and America.

Electricity
220 volts AC (and 110 too in some hotels), 50 cycles. European Continental-type plugs in old buildings, Australian 3-pin flat-type in the new. Adaptors can be purchased locally for either type (ie from new 3-pin to old 2-pin and vice versa). Best to bring a universal adapter for British 3-pin plugs, as these are not available in Argentina.

Embassies and consulates
Visit www.mrecic.gov.ar, for a full list of embassies.

Greetings
Argentines are extremely courteous and friendly people, and start every interaction, no matter how small, with a greeting. You'll be welcomed in shops and ticket offices too. Take the time to respond with a smile and a *Buenos días* or *Hola* in return. Argentines are sociable people, and haven't yet lost the art of passing the time of day – you'll be considered a bit abrupt if you don't too. As you leave, say *Chau* (bye) or *Hasta luego* (see you later). Strangers are generally treated with great kindness and generosity and your warmth in return will be greatly appreciated.

If you're introduced to new people or friends, you'll be kissed, once, on the right cheek as you say hello and goodbye. This sometimes goes for men to men too, if they're friends (although it's more of a touching of cheeks than a kiss). In a business or official context, Argentines tend to be formal, and very polite.

Health
See your GP or travel clinic at least 6 weeks before departure for general advice on travel risks and vaccinations. Try phoning a specialist travel clinic if your own doctor is unfamiliar with health conditions in Argentina. Make sure you have sufficient medical travel insurance, get a dental check, know your own blood group and if you suffer a long-term condition such as diabetes or epilepsy, obtain a Medic Alert bracelet/ necklace (www.medicalert.co.uk). If you wear glasses, take a copy of your prescription.

Vaccinations and anti-malarials
Vaccinations for tetanus, hepatitis A, typhoid, yellow fever and, following the 2009 outbreak, influenza A (H1N1) are commonly recommended for Argentina. Sometimes advised are vaccines for hepatitis B and rabies. The final decision, however, should be based on a consultation with your GP or travel clinic. You should also confirm your primary courses and boosters are up to date.

Malaria is a substantial risk in parts of north and northeastern Argentina.

Specialist advice should be taken on the best anti- malarials to use.

Health risks The most common cause of travellers' **diarrhoea** is from eating contaminated food. Be wary of salads (what were they washed in, who handled them), re-heated foods or food that has been left out in the sun having been cooked earlier in the day. There is a simple adage that says wash it, peel it, boil it or forget it. It is also standard advice to be careful with water and ice. Ask yourself where the water came from. If you have any doubts then boil it or filter and treat it. Tap water in the major cities is in theory safe to drink but it may be advisable to err on the side of caution and drink only bottled or boiled water. Avoid having ice in drinks unless you trust that it is from a reliable source.There are many filter/ treatment devices now available on the market. Swimming in sea or river water that has been contaminated by sewage can also be a cause; ask locally if it is safe. **Diarrhoea** may be also caused by viruses, bacteria (such as E-coli), protozoal (such as giardia), salmonella and cholera. It may be accompanied by vomiting or by severe abdominal pain. Any kind of diarrhoea responds well to the replacement of water and salts. Sachets of rehydration salts can be bought in most chemists and can be dissolved in boiled water. If the symptoms persist, consult a doctor.

Travelling in high altitudes can bring on **altitude sickness**. On reaching heights above 3000 m, the heart may start pounding and the traveller may experience shortness of breath. Smokers and those with underlying heart or lung disease are often hardest hit. Take it easy for the first few days, rest and drink plenty of water – you will feel better soon. It is essential to get acclimatized before undertaking long treks or arduous activities.

Mosquitoes are more of a nuisance than a serious hazard but some, of course, are carriers of serious diseases such as **malaria**, so it is sensible to avoid being bitten as much as possible. Sleep off the ground and use a mosquito net and some kind of insecticide. Mosquito coils release insecticide as they burn and are available in many shops, as are tablets of insecticide, which are placed on a heated mat plugged into a wall socket.

If you get sick Contact your embassy or consulate for a list of doctors and dentists who speak your language, or at least some English. Doctors and health facilities in major cities are also listed in the Directory sections of this book. Good-quality healthcare is available in the larger centres of Argentina but it can be expensive, especially hospitalization. Make sure you have adequate insurance (see below).

Useful websites
www.btha.org British Travel Health Association.
www.cdc.gov US government site that gives excellent advice on travel health and details of disease outbreaks.
www.fco.gov.uk British Foreign and Commonwealth Office travel site has useful information on each country, people, climate and a list of UK embassies/consulates.
www.fitfortravel.scot.nhs.uk A-Z of vaccine/health advice for each country.
www.numberonehealth.co.uk Travel screening services, vaccine and travel health advice, email/SMS text vaccine reminders and screens returned travellers for tropical diseases.

Money ➔ *US$1 = Arg $4.16, £1 = Arg $6.83, €1 = Arg $6 (Aug 2011).*
Currency The unit of currency is the Argentine peso (Arg $), divided into 100 centavos. Peso notes in circulation are 2, 5, 10, 20, 50 and 100. Coins in circulation are 5, 10, 25 and 50 centavos and 1 peso. Most

major towns have exchange places (*casas de cambio*), and exchange rates are quoted in major newspapers daily. Also see www.xe.com, for up-to-date rates. There is a severe shortage of coins in Argentina, and you will find that hardly anyone can break large notes. Use them in supermarkets, restaurants and hotels, and take out odd amounts from the bank like $190 pesos instead of $200 pesos.

Cost of travelling Argentina's economy has picked up since the 2001 economic crisis, but prices have risen steeply, particularly for hotels and tourist services. Nevertheless, you'll still find Argentina a very economical country to travel around.

You can find comfortable accommodation with a private bathroom and breakfast for around US$50 for 2 people, while a good dinner in the average restaurant will be around US$10-15 per person. Prices are much cheaper away from the main touristy areas: El Calafate, Ushuaia and Buenos Aires can be particularly pricey. For travellers on a budget, hostels usually cost US$10-13 per person in a shared dorm. Cheap breakfasts can be found in any ordinary café for around US$4, and there are cheap set meals for lunchtime at many restaurants, costing around US$7, US$8 in Buenos Aires. Camping costs vary widely, but expect to pay no more than US$3-6 per tent – usually less. Long-distance bus travel on major routes is very cheap, and it's well worth splashing out an extra 20% for *coche cama* service on overnight journeys.

Credit and debit cards By far the easiest way to get cash while you're in Argentina is to use a credit card at an ATM (*cajero automático*). These can be found in every town or city (with the notable exception of El Chaltén in the south) and most accept all major cards, with Visa and MasterCard being the most widely accepted in small places. The rate of exchange is that which applies at the moment the money is withdrawn and commission is usually around 2-3%, but check with your credit card company before leaving home. Note that Argentine ATMs give you your cash and receipt before the card is returned: don't walk away without the card, as many travellers are reported to have done. Credit cards are now accepted almost everywhere as payment but you will need to show your passport together with the card. It's a good idea to carry cash to pay in cheaper shops, restaurants and hotels, and some places will give a discount for cash. Note that when taking money out of the ATM, Banelco machines have a limit of $320 pesos per withdrawal and $1000 pesos per day. Link machines permit more than that, $600 pesos, and $1200 pesos per day. This can be very frustrating so try paying for hotels and tours on credit card if you can. MasterCard emergency number is T0800-555 0507 and Visa is T0800-32222.

Traveller's cheques There's little point in carrying traveller's cheques in Argentina since there are exchange facilities only in big towns, and commission is very high: usually 10%. A passport is essential and you may have to show proof of purchase, so transactions can take a long time. Traveller's cheques also attract thieves and though you can of course arrange a refund, the process will hold up your travel plans. Far better to bring your debit card and withdraw money from ATMs.

Transfers Transfers are almost impossible: money can be transferred between banks but you'll need to find out which local bank is related to your own (normally none) and give all the relevant information with the routing codes. Allow 2-3 days; cash is usually paid in pesos and is subject to tax. For Western Union in Argentina, T011-4322-7774.

Opening hours

Business hours Banks, government offices and businesses are usually open Mon-Fri 0800-1300 in summer, and Mon-Fri 1000-1500 in winter. Some businesses open again in the evening, 1700-2000. **Cafés and restaurants**: cafés are busy from 2400. Restaurants are open for lunch 1230-1500, dinner 2100-2400. **Nightclubs**: open at 2400, but usually only get busy around 0200. **Post offices**: often open *corrido* – don't close for lunch or siesta. **Shops**: in Buenos Aires most are open 0900-1800. Elsewhere, everything closes for siesta 1300-1700.

Safety

Relatively speaking, Buenos Aires is one of the safest cities in South America, and Argentina as a whole is an easy and safe place to travel, but that doesn't mean you need to drop your guard altogether. There are a few simple things you can do to avoid being a victim of crime.

Fake money There is a big problem with fake notes in Argentina. The best way to tell if your money is not a fake is to look for the following 3 things: the green numbers showing the value of the note (on the left hand top corner) should shine, or shimmer; if you hold the note up to the sky you should see a watermark; lastly there should be a continuous line from the top of the note to the bottom about ¾ of the way along (also when held up to the light). The most common fake notes are $100 pesos, $20 pesos and $10 pesos. Some taxi drivers reportedly circulate fakes late at night with drunk passengers, or you may be given them back in change in markets and fairs. Check the notes thoroughly before walking away. Try to break large notes in hostels/hotels or supermarkets to avoid being given a fake in change.

Places to avoid In most towns the train and bus stations should be avoided late at night

and early in the morning. If you arrive at that time, try to arrange for your hotel or hostel to pick you up. If you can, in Buenos Aires and when you are travelling, visit the bus station to buy your tickets the day before so you can find out where the platform is and where you need to go. Also watch your belongings being stowed in the boot of the bus, and keep the ticket you'll be given since you'll need it to claim your luggage on arrival.

Precautions Some general tips are: don't walk along the street with your map or guidebook in hand – check where you are going beforehand and duck into shops to have a quick look at your map. In cafés make sure you have your handbag on your lap or your backpack strap around your ankles. Try not to wear clothes that stand out, and certainly don't wear expensive rings, watches or jewellery that shines. Remember that the people around you don't know that you bought that watch for US$10 second hand – to them it looks expensive. Always catch Radio Taxis ask at your hostel/hotel the best taxi company to use and their direct number. When in a taxi, if possible lock the doors, or ask the driver to.

And finally, just remember the golden rules: store your money and credit cards in small amounts in different places in your luggage; scan and email yourself copies of your passport, visas and insurance forms; and keep an eye on the news or newspapers to be aware of what is happening in the country that you are travelling in.

If you are the victim of a **sexual assault**, you are advised in the first instance to contact a doctor (this can be your home doctor if you prefer). You will need tests to determine whether you have contracted any sexually transmitted diseases; you may also need advice on post-coital contraception. You should also contact your embassy, where consular staff are very willing to help in cases of assault. For more advice see

www. dailystrength. org and
www.rapecrisis.org.uk.

Scams Be aware of scams. There are 2
favoured scams in use. One is that someone
will discreetly spill a liquid on you, then a
'helpful stranger' will draw your attention to it
and offer to help you clean it off. Meanwhile
someone else has raided your pockets or run
off with your bags. If someone does point out
something on your clothes, keep walking until
you see a coffee shop and clean up there. The
second scam involves someone driving past
you on a motorbike, ripping your bag off your
shoulders, and driving away off into the sunset.
To avoid this, wear your bag with the strap
over your head and one shoulder and keep
your bag on the opposite side of your body to
the street. If travelling with a laptop, don't use a
computer bag. Buy a satchel or handbag big
enough to carry it in.

Taxis
Always take Radio Taxis. Ask your hostel or
hotel for a reputable company and call them
whenever you need a taxi. They generally
take only around 10 mins to come. Always
lock the doors in the taxi as taxi doors have
reportedly been opened at traffic
intersections when the car is stationary.

Tax
Airport tax   US$28 to be paid on all
international flights exiting the country,
except to Montevideo from Aeroparque
Airport, which is subject to US$14 tax. Airport
tax can be prepaid, and you should check if
it's included in your ticket when you book.
Internal flights are subject to US$12, included
in your ticket everywhere but the airport at El
Calafate, where you must pay in pesos. When
in transit from one international flight to
another, you may be obliged to pass through
immigration and customs, have your
passport stamped and be made to pay an
airport tax on departure. There is a 5% tax on
the purchase of air tickets. There is now an
entry fee for Argentina, see page 7.

VAT   21%; VAT is not levied on medicines,
books and some foodstuffs.

Telephone → *Country code +54.*
Ringing: equal tones with long pauses.
Engaged: equal tones with equal pauses.
  Phoning in Argentina is made very easy
by the abundance of *locutorios* – phone
centres with private booths where you can
talk for as long as you like, and pay
afterwards, the price appearing on a small
screen in your booth. There's no need for
change or phonecards, and *locutorios* often
have internet, photocopying and fax
services.
  An alternative to *locutorios* is to buy a
phonecard and use it from your hostel or
hotel. 2 good brands are **Argentina Global**
and **Hable Mas**, available from *kioskos* and
locutorios for 5 or 10 pesos. Dial the free
0800 number on the card, and a code
(which you scratch the card to reveal), and
you can phone anywhere in the world. For
US$3 you can talk for 1 hr internationally.
Call from your hotel/hostel, as it only is the
cost of a local call. These can sometimes be
used in *locutorios* too, though the rates are
higher, and sometimes from your hotel
room, ask reception. Otherwise Skype,
www.skpye. com, is the cheapest way to
keep in touch.

Time
GMT -3.

Tipping
10% in restaurants and cafés. Porters and
ushers are usually tipped. Tipping isn't
obligatory, but it is appreciated.

Visas and immigration
Visas on entry
Passports are not required by citizens of

neighbouring countries who hold identity cards issued by their own governments. Visas are not necessary for US citizens, British citizens and nationals of other Western European countries, plus Australia, Barbados, Bolivia, Brazil, Canada, Chile, Colombia, Costa Rica, Croatia, Czech Republic, Dominican Republic, Ecuador, El Salvador, Guatemala, Haiti, Honduras, Hungary, Israel, Jamaica, Japan, Malaysia, Mexico, New Zealand, Nicaragua, Panama, Paraguay, Peru, Poland, Singapore, Slovenia, South Africa, Turkey, Uruguay and Venezuela. Visitors from these countries are given a tourist card on entry and may stay for 3 months. There is an entry fee, however, for details see page 7.

For visitors from all other countries, there are 3 types of visa: a business 'temporary' visa (US$35, valid 1 year), a tourist visa (US$35 approximately, fees may change), and a transit visa. Tourist visas are usually valid for 3 months and are multiple entry.

Visa extensions and renewals

All visitors can renew their tourist visas for another 3 months by going in person to the **National Directorate of Migration**, Antártida Argentina 1365, Buenos Aires, T011-4312 8663 (ring first to check opening times), and paying a fee of US$35: ask for *Prorrogas de Permanencia*. No renewals are given after the expiry date. Alternatively, for a 90-day extension of your stay in Argentina, just leave the country at any land border, and you'll get another 3 month tourist visa stamped in your passport on return. Alternatively, you can forego all the paper-work by paying a US$45 fine at a border immigration post (queues are shorter than in Buenos Aires, but still allow 30 mins). The most popular way of renewing your visa from Buenos Aires is to spend the day in Uruguay, which is only 45 mins away by boat.

Advice and tips

All visitors are advised to carry their passports at all times, and it is illegal not to have identification handy. In practice, though, this is not advisable. Photocopy your passport twice, carry 1 copy, and scan your passport and email it to yourself for emergencies. You'll often be asked for your passport number, when checking into hotels and if paying by credit card, so learn it off by heart. The police like searching backpackers at border points: remain calm – this is a normal procedure. If you are staying in the country for several weeks, it may be worthwhile registering at your embassy or consulate. This will help if your passport is stolen as the process of replacing it is simplified and speeded up.

Weights and measures

The metric system is used in Argentina.

Contents

Footprint features

Ins and outs

Orientation

→ Phone code 011. Population 2,776,138 (Greater Buenos Aires 12,046,799).

The city of Buenos Aires is situated just inland from the docks on the south bank of the Río de la Plata. The formal city centre is around **Plaza de Mayo**, where the historical **Cabildo** faces the florid pink presidential palace, the **Casa Rosada**, from whose balcony presidents have appealed to their people, and where the people have historically come to protest. From here, the broad Parisian-style boulevard of the **Avenida de Mayo** leads to the seat of government at the wonderfully imposing **Congreso de la Nación**, lined with marvellous buildings from the city's own belle époque, including the theatrical **Café Tortoni** ① *www.cafetortoni.com.ar*, built in 1858 and frequented by Argentine writer Jorges Luis Borges. Halfway, it crosses the widest street in the world, the 18 lanes of roaring **Avenida 9 de Julio**, a main artery leading south, with its mighty central obelisk and the splendid Teatro Colón (which has recently undergone a multi-million dollar makeover).

The main shopping streets are found north of Plaza de Mayo, along the popular pedestrianized **Florida**, which leads to the elegant and leafy Plaza San Martín. This central area is easy to walk around and you can buy everything from chic leather bags to cheap CDs, with lots of banks, internet cafés and *locutorios* (phone centres).

Just west of the centre, crossing Avenida 9 de Julio, is the smart upmarket suburb or *barrio* of **Recoleta** where wealthy *Porteños* (Buenos Aires' residents) live in large apartment blocks with doormen and gold door handles; you'll find most of the city's finest museums here, as well as the famous **Recoleta Cemetery**, where Evita Perón was finally buried. Just outside the cemetery, there's a busy craft market at weekends, innumerable cafés and bars, and the chic **Buenos Aires Design**, an upmarket shopping centre filled with exclusive products. Further north still, via the elegant green parks of **Palermo**, with its zoo, wonderfully shaped planetarium and botanical garden, is the fabulous *barrio* of **Palermo Viejo**. This is *the* place to hang out in Buenos Aires, and a relaxing place to shop, as you stroll leafy cobbled streets past 1920s buildings and browse in cool designer clothes and interiors shops. The whole area is alive with bars and excellent restaurants, and there are fabulous places to stay in Palermo Viejo, and neighbouring Palermo Soho too, making it possible to avoid the city centre altogether if you want a quieter visit.

Puerto Madero has become the most popular place to eat close to the centre, with busy upmarket restaurants and luxury hotels filling the handsome brick warehouses on the stylishly renovated docks area. This is a good place to go for an early evening drink, and to stroll past old sailing ships and painted cranes. Further south, the green spaces of the **Costanera Sur** are busy in summer with *Porteños* relaxing, groups of friends sipping *mate* or barbecuing steak. Here there's a **Reserva Ecológica** where you could retreat for some inner city wildlife, and walk or cycle for a couple of hours. Just inland, the city's most atmospheric *barrio* is irresistible **San Telmo**, once the city's centre, with narrow streets where cafés and antique markets are tucked away in the attractively crumbling 1900s buildings. Now the area is a lively and bohemian artistic centre with a popular market in the quaint Plaza Dorrego and along the cobbled street of Defensa on Sundays, where tango is danced for tourists among stalls selling silver, plates and bric-a-brac. Nightlife is lively here, but you'll also want to explore the city's tasty restaurants in Recoleta, Palermo, or the Las Cañitas area in between the two.

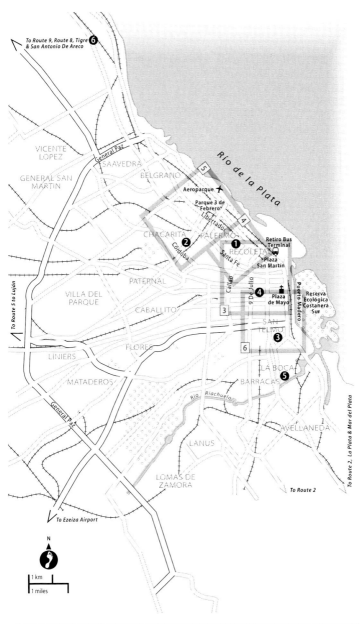

To Route 9, Route 8, Tigre & San Antonio De Areco

VICENTE LÓPEZ

GENERAL SAN MARTÍN

SAAVEDRA

General Paz

BELGRANO

Río de la Plata

Aeroparque

Parque 3 de Febrero

CHACARITA

PALERMO

Córdoba

Libertador

Santa Fe

RECOLETA

Retiro Bus Terminal

Plaza San Martín

PATERNAL

VILLA DEL PARQUE

CABALLITO

Callao

9 De Julio

Plaza de Mayo

Puerto Madero

Reserva Ecológica Costanera Sur

To Route 5 to Luján

FLORES

LINIERS

SAN TELMO

MATADEROS

BARRACAS

LA BOCA

Río Riachuelo

General Paz

AVELLANEDA

To Route 2, La Plata & Mar del Plata

LANÚS

To Route 2

LOMAS DE ZAMORA

To Ezeiza Airport

N

1 km

1 miles

Street layout

Streets are organized on a regular grid pattern, with blocks numbered in groups of one hundred. It's easy to find an address, since street numbers start from the dock side/the river rising from east to west, and north/south streets are numbered starting from Avenida Rivadavia, one block north of Avenida de Mayo, and rise in both directions. Juan D Perón used to be called Cangallo, and Scalabrini Ortiz used to be Canning (the old names are sometimes still referred to). Avenida Roque Sáenz Peña and Avenida Julio A Roca are commonly referred to as Diagonal Norte and Diagonal Sur respectively.

Background

Buenos Aires was officially founded in 1536 by Pedro de Mendoza acting on orders from his Spanish King. A small fort was built (most researchers place the fort closer to modern

② Metro (Subte)

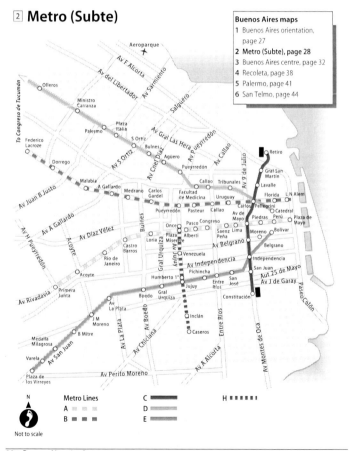

Buenos Aires maps
1 Buenos Aires orientation, page 27
2 Metro (Subte), page 28
3 Buenos Aires centre, page 32
4 Recoleta, page 38
5 Palermo, page 41
6 San Telmo, page 44

day San Isidro north of the current-day city), and a small band of settlers were left to eke out a living. The settlement failed after a few precious years and it was left up to Juan de Garay (who has a street named after him in San Telmo, it was in fact the first official street of the city) 40 odd years later, in 1580, to found – for the second time – the city he named Ciudad de la Santísima Trinidad y Puerto de Nuestra Señora del Buen Ayre. Not surprisingly, the name in its entirety, didn't stick. It was shortened to Santa María del Buen Aire, then shortened again to simply Buenos Aires.

However, in present day Buenos Aires nothing remains of this early settlement, which also didn't take off as a city for some 200 years. It has none of the colonial splendour of Salta (in the northwest of Argentina), because while Salta was by that time a busy administrative centre on the main trade route for silver and mules from the main Spanish colony of Alto Perú, Santa María del Buen Aire, the city of the 'good winds', was left to fester, her port used only for a roaring trade in contraband. Later on Jesuits came and built schools, churches and the country's first university in what is now San Telmo, a legacy left in the wonderful Manzana de las Luces, which you can still explore today.

In 1776 Buenos Aires became Viceroyalty of the Río de la Plata area, putting it firmly on the map for trade, and the city's strategic position on this estuary brought wealth and progress. Two invasions by the British for control of the port in 1806 and 1807 were quickly quelled but sparked a surge for independence in the burgeoning Argentine nation. There is a street in San Telmo called Defensa that marks the limit of where the British soldiers reached, when residents were ordered by the army, lacking in weapons, to pour boiling oil from the building tops to stop the invasion. Hence the name Defensa – defence. After separating from Spain in 1816, Buenos Aires became its new capital, giving the Porteños a further sense of pride.

By 1914, Buenos Aires was rightfully regarded as the most important city in South America. The wealth generated from the vast fertile Pampas, inhabited by the immigrants from Europe was manifested in the flamboyant architecture you see in Teatro Colón, Avenida de Mayo and the palaces of Recoleta. Massive waves of immigration from Italy and Spain had arrived in Buenos Aires in the late 19th century, creating the characteristic Argentine identity, and the language described most accurately as Spanish spoken by Italians. The tango was born in the port areas of the city, music filled with nostalgia for the places left behind, and currently enjoying a revival among 20-somethings, who fill the milongas, breathing new passion into old steps. Now, nearly a third of the country's 36 million inhabitants live in Gran Buenos Aires, in the sprawling conurbation that stretches west from the smart areas of Palermo, Martínez, and upmarket San Isidro, to the poorer Avellaneda and La Matanza. Shanty towns, called villas, surround the city and the most famous Villa 31 can be seen behind Retiro bus station in the centre, which you will see if you catch any long distance bus. It is all part of the colourful stew of Buenos Aires' life. It is truly one of the world's great cities, and a fine start to your trip to Argentina.

City centre

Plaza de Mayo

This broad open plaza is both the historic heart of the city, and its centre of power, since it's surrounded by some of the city's most important public buildings. Just behind the Plaza de Mayo were the city's original docks, where Argentina's wealth was built on exporting meat and leather from the Pampas. All the country's powers are gathered nearby, and the Plaza remains the symbolic political centre of the city. Most famously, there's pink Casa de Gobierno or **Casa Rosada** ①*Bolívar 65, T011-4334 1782, tours Sun 1400-1800, guided tours 1500 and 1630, free*, which lies on the east side, looking out towards the Río Plata, and contains the offices of the president of the Argentine Republic. The changing of the guards takes place every two hours from 0700-1900.

The decision to paint the seat of government pink resulted from President Sarmiento's (1868-1874) desire to symbolize national unity by blending the colours of the rival factions that had fought each other for much of the 19th century: the Federalists (red) and the Unitarians (white). The colour itself was originally derived from a mixture of lime and ox blood and fat, to render the surface impermeable. The Plaza has been the site of many historic events: Perón and Evita frequently appeared on its balcony before the masses gathered on the plaza, at one point the military (opposed to Perón) bombed it, and when the economy crumbled in December 2001, angry crowds of *cacerolazas* (including middle-class ladies banging their *cazerolas*, or saucepans) demonstrated outside, together with angry mobs. Since 1977, the Mothers and now, Grandmothers, of the Plaza de Mayo (*Madres y Abuelas de la Plaza de Mayo*), www.madres.org, have marched in silent remembrance of their children who disappeared during the 'Dirty Wa'. Every Thursday at 1530, they march anti-clockwise around the central monument with photos of their disappeared loved-ones pinned to their chests. It is a moving sight. On the plaza, there are statues of General Belgrano in front of the Casa Rosada and of Columbus, behind the Casa Rosada in the Parque Colón. The guided tours of the Casa de Gobierno allow you to see its statuary and the rich furnishing of its halls and its libraries.

Opposite the Casa Rosada, on the west side of the plaza, is the white-columned **Cabildo**, which has been rebuilt several times since the original structure was erected in the 18th century; most recently the façade in 1940. Inside, where the movement for independence from Spain was first planned, is the **Museo del Cabildo y la Revolución** ① *Bolívar 65, T011-4334 1782, Tue-Fri 1030-1700, Sun 1130-1800, US$1*, which has just been renovated. Inside is worth a visit, especially for the paintings of old Buenos Aires, the documents and maps recording the May 1810 revolution, and memorabilia of the British attacks, as well as Jesuit art. In the patio is a café and stalls selling handicrafts (Thursday-Friday 1100-1800).

Many of the centre's most important buildings date from after 1776 when Buenos Aires underwent a big change, becoming the capital of the new viceroyalty and the official port. The **Catedral Metropolitana** ① *Rivadavia 437, T011-4331 2845, Mon-Fri 0800-1900, Sat-Sun 0900-1930, guided visits Sat and Sun at 1630 (San Martín's mausoleum and crypt) and 1315 (religious art), and daily at 1530 (temple and crypt), Mass held daily, check for times*, on the north side of the plaza, lies on the site of the first church in Buenos Aires, built in 1580. The current structure was built in French neoclassical style between 1758 and 1807, and inside, in the right-hand aisle, guarded by soldiers in fancy uniforms, is the imposing tomb of General José de San Martín (1778-1850), Argentina's greatest hero who liberated the country from the Spanish.

Just east of the cathedral, the **Banco de la Nación** is regarded as one of the great works of the famous architect Alejandro Bustillo (who designed the wonderful **Hotel Llao Llao** in Bariloche). Built in 1940-1955, its central hall is topped by a marble dome 50 m in diameter. Take in all these buildings, and you become aware that the banks, political and religious institutions, together with the military headquarters opposite, are all gathered in one potent place. No wonder then that people always come here to demonstrate.

Downtown: La City

Just north of Plaza de Mayo, between 25 de Mayo and the pedestrianized Florida, lies the main banking district known as La City, with some handsome buildings to admire. The **Banco de Boston** ① *Florida 99 and Av RS Peña*, dates from 1924, and while there are no guided visits, you can walk inside during banking hours to appreciate its lavish ceiling and marble interior (no cameras allowed). There's also the marvellous art-deco **Banco de la Provincia de Buenos Aires**, at San Martín 137, built in 1940, and the **Bolsa de Comercio**, at 25 de Mayo and Sarmiento, which dates from 1916 and houses the stock exchange, but visits aren't permitted. The **Banco Hipotecario** (formerly the Bank of London and South America), corner Reconquista and B Mitre, was designed by SEPRA (Santiago Sánchez Elia, Federico Peralta Ramos, and Alfredo Agostini). It was completed in 1963, in bold 'brutalist' design. You can visit during banking hours.

The **Basílica Nuestra Señora de La Merced** ① *J D Perón and Reconquista 207, Mon-Fri 0800-1800*, founded in 1604 and rebuilt 1760-1769, was used as a command post in 1807 by Argentine troops resisting the British invasion. Its highly decorated interior has an altar with an 18th-century wooden figure of Christ, the work of indigenous carvers from Misiones, and it has one of the few fine carillons of bells in Buenos Aires. A craft fair is held on Thursday and Friday 1100-1900. Next door, at Reconquista 269, is the **Convento de la Merced**, originally built in 1601 but reconstructed in the 18th and 19th centuries with a peaceful courtyard in its cloisters.

There are a few rather dry museums here, purely for historians: **Museo Numismático Dr José Evaristo Uriburu**, in the Banco Central library, tells the history of the country through its currency; **Museo y Biblioteca Mitre** ① *San Martín 336, T011-4394 8240, www.museomitre.gov.ar, Mon-Fri 1400-1730 (library and archives only on Wed), US$1.50*, preserves intact the colonial-style home of President Bartolomé Mitre (1862-1868). More interesting and accessible is the bizarre **Museo de la Policía Federal** ① *San Martín 353, floors 8 and 9, T011-4394 6857, Tue-Fri 1400-1800, closed Jan and Feb*, which portrays the fascinating history of crime in the city, and includes a gruesome forensic section, definitely not for the squeamish. Information on museums can be found at www.museosargentinos.org.ar (in English).

South of Plaza de Mayo

To the southwest of the Plaza de Mayo, towards San Telmo, there is an entire block of buildings built by the Jesuits between 1622 and 1767, called the **Manzana de las Luces** (Enlightenment Square) – bounded by streets Moreno, Alsina, Perú and Bolívar. The former Jesuit church of **San Ignacio de Loyola** (see below for tours), begun in 1664, is the oldest colonial building in Buenos Aires and the best example of the baroque architecture introduced by the Jesuits (renovated in the 18th and 19th centuries), with splendid golden naves dating from 1710-1734 (www.manzanadelasluces.gov.ar). Also in this block are the **Colegio Nacional de Buenos Aires** ① *Bolívar 263, T011-4331 0734, www.cnba.uba.ar*, formerly the Jesuits' Colegio Máximo in the 18th century, and now the city's most prestigious secondary school. Below these buildings are **18th-century tunnels** ① *T011-4342 4655*. These are thought to have been used by the Jesuits for escape

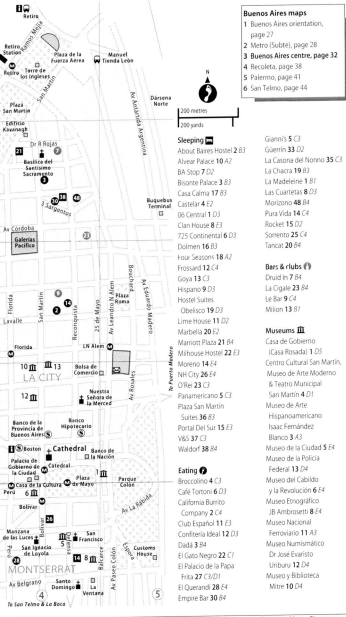

Buenos Aires maps

1 Buenos Aires orientation, page 27
2 Metro (Subte), page 28
3 Buenos Aires centre, page 32
4 Recoleta, page 38
5 Palermo, page 41
6 San Telmo, page 44

Sleeping 🛏

About Baires Hostel **2** *B3*
Alvear Palace **10** *A2*
BA Stop **7** *D2*
Bisonte Palace **3** *B3*
Casa Calma **17** *B3*
Castelar **4** *E2*
06 Central **1** *D3*
Clan House **8** *E3*
725 Continental **6** *D3*
Dolmen **16** *B3*
Four Seasons **18** *A2*
Frossard **12** *C4*
Goya **13** *C3*
Hispano **9** *D3*
Hostel Suites
  Obelisco **19** *D3*
Lime House **11** *D2*
Marbella **20** *E2*
Marriott Plaza **21** *B4*
Milhouse Hostel **22** *E3*
Moreno **14** *E4*
NH City **26** *E4*
O'Rei **23** *C3*
Panamericano **5** *C3*
Plaza San Martín
  Suites **36** *B3*
Portal Del Sur **15** *E3*
V&S **37** *C3*
Waldorf **38** *B4*

Eating 🍴

Broccolino **4** *C3*
Café Tortoni **6** *D3*
California Burrito
  Company **2** *C4*
Club Español **11** *E3*
Confitería Ideal **12** *D3*
Dadá **3** *B4*
El Gato Negro **22** *C1*
El Palacio de la Papa
  Frita **27** *C3/D1*
El Querandí **28** *E4*
Empire Bar **30** *B4*

Gianni's **5** *C3*
Güerrín **33** *D2*
La Casona del Nonno **35** *C3*
La Chacra **19** *B3*
La Madeleine **1** *B1*
Las Cuartetas **8** *D3*
Morizono **48** *B4*
Pura Vida **14** *C4*
Rocket **15** *D2*
Sorrento **25** *C4*
Tancat **20** *B4*

Bars & clubs 🍸

Druid In **7** *B4*
La Cigale **23** *B4*
Le Bar **9** *C4*
Milion **13** *B1*

Museums 🏛

Casa de Gobierno
  (Casa Rosada) **1** *D5*
Centro Cultural San Martín,
  Museo de Arte Moderno
  & Teatro Municipal
  San Martín **4** *D1*
Museo de Arte
  Hispanoamericano
  Isaac Fernández
  Blanco **3** *A3*
Museo de la Ciudad **5** *E4*
Museo de la Policía
  Federal **13** *D4*
Museo del Cabildo
  y la Revolución **6** *E4*
Museo Etnográfico
  JB Ambrosetti **8** *E4*
Museo Nacional
  Ferroviario **11** *A3*
Museo Numismático
  Dr José Evaristo
  Uriburu **12** *D4*
Museo y Biblioteca
  Mitre **10** *D4*

or for smuggling contraband from the port. For centuries the whole block was the centre of intellectual activity, and although little remains to see today, the history is fascinating. All **guided tours** ⓘ *from Perú 272, Mon-Fri 1500, Sat-Sun 1500, 1630, 1800 (Mon 1300 free tour) in Spanish (in English by prior arrangement), arrive 15 mins before tour, US$2*, explore the tunnels; only weekend tours include San Ignacio and Colegio Nacional.

Museo de la Ciudad ⓘ *Alsina 412, T011-4343 2123, www.museos.buenosaires.gov.ar/ ciudad.htm, Mon-Sun, 1100-1900, US$1, free on Mon and Wed*, is worth visiting for an insight into 19th-century Buenos Aires life. The historical house includes a 1900s chemist's shop, Farmacia La Estrella, and has a permanent exhibition covering social history and popular culture, with special exhibitions on daily life in Buenos Aires. The **Church of San Francisco** ⓘ *Alsina and Defensa, Mon-Fri 0700-1300, 1500-1900, guided visits Tue 1530 and 1630, Sat 1630 and 1730*, was built by the Franciscan Order in 1730-1754 and given a new façade in 1911 in German baroque style. There's a fine baroque pulpit and the chapel of San Roque.

Argentina has a rich heritage from numerous indigenous groups that inhabited the country before the Spanish arrived, and their history is well-charted in the anthropological museum **Museo Etnográfico J B Ambrosetti** ⓘ *1 block south of the San Francisco church at Moreno 350, T011-4345 8196, www.museoetnografico.filo.uba.ar, Tue-Fri 1300-1900, Sat-Sun 1500-1900 (closed in Jan), US$0.70, guided visits Sat-Sun 1600*. Displays are limited, but very well laid out, and include some fascinating treasures, such as Inca textiles and ceramics, and Bolivian and Mapuche silverwork, all in an attractive building dating from 1880.

One block further south at Defensa and Belgrano, the **Church of Santo Domingo**, ⓘ *Mon-Fri 0900-1300, Sun 1000-1200, no tours offered*, was founded in 1751. During the British attack on Buenos Aires in 1806 some of the British soldiers took refuge in the church and it was bombarded by local forces. Look out for the huge wooden cannon balls embedded in the towers on the outside: fakes, sadly. The British flags inside are worth seeing, and General Belgrano, a major figure in Argentine independence, is buried here.

Avenida de Mayo to Congreso

From Plaza de Mayo, take a stroll down this broad leafy avenue which links the Casa Rosada to the Congress building to the west. The avenue was built between 1889 and 1894, inspired by the grand design of Paris, and filled with elaborate French baroque and art nouveau buildings. At Perú and Avenida de Mayo is the **Subte station Perú**, furnished by the Museo de la Ciudad to resemble its original state, with posters and furniture of the time. You'll need to buy a US$0.30 ticket to have a look, or take a train.

Along the avenue west from here, you'll see the splendid French-style **Casa de la Cultura** at number 575, home of the newspaper *La Prensa*, which is topped with bronze statues. At No 702 is the fine Parisian-style **Edificio Drabble**, and at No 769, the elegant **Palacio Vera**, from 1910. Argentina's most celebrated writer, Jorge Luis Borges, was fond of the many cafés that once filled Avenida de Mayo, of which **Café Tortoni** ⓘ *www.cafetortoni.com.ar*, at No 825, is the most famous in Buenos Aires and the haunt of many illustrious writers, artists and poets since 1858. Its high ceilings with ornate plaster work and art nouveau stained glass, tall columns and elegant mirrors plunge you straight back into another era. It's an atmospheric place for coffee, but particularly wonderful for the poetry recitals, tango and live music, which are still performed here in the evenings. There are also plenty of places nearby for a quick lunch, and lots of cheap hotels.

Continuing west over Avenida 9 de Julio, there's the superb 1928 **Hotel Castelar** ⓘ *www.castelarhotel.com.ar*, at No 1152, still open (see Sleeping, page 47), and retaining its former glory, as is the beautiful art nouveau **Hotel Chile**, at No 1297. At the western end of the avenue is the astounding **Palacio Barola** ⓘ *No 1370, www.pbarolo.com.ar, guided tours Mon and Thu 1400 and 1800, book tours in English, US$8, T011-1550 279 035, barolotours@gmail.com*, built by a textile magnate in 1923 with architectural details inspired by the Italian poet Dante. Avenida de Mayo culminates on the **Plaza del Congreso**, with the **congress building** ⓘ *T011-4953 3081, ext 3885 for guided visits, Mon, Tue Thu, Fri 1100, 1700, 1900*, in Italian academic style, housing the country's government.

Plaza San Martín and Retiro

Ten blocks north of the Plaza de Mayo, and just south of **Retiro station**, is the splendid Plaza San Martín, on a hill originally marking the northern limit of the city. It has since been designed by Argentina's famous landscape architect Charles Thays, and is filled with luxuriant mature palms and plane trees. It is popular with runners in the early morning, as well as office workers at lunchtimes. At the western corner is an equestrian **statue of San Martín** (1862), and at the northern end of the plaza is the **Malvinas memorial** with elaborately dressed guards and an eternal flame to those who fell in the Falklands/ Malvinas War, 1982.

Around the plaza are several elegant mansions, among them the **Palacio San Martín**, designed in 1909 in French academic style for the wealthy Anchorena family, and now occupied by the Ministry of Foreign Affairs. Most striking is the elegant art deco **Edificio Kavanagh**, east of the plaza, which was the tallest building in South America when completed in 1936. Behind it is the **Basílica del Santísimo Sacramento** (1916), the church favoured by wealthy *Porteños*.

The **Plaza de la Fuerza Aérea**, northeast of Plaza San Martín, was until 1982 called the Plaza Británica; in the centre is a clock tower presented by British and Anglo-Argentine residents in 1916, still known as the Torre de los Ingleses.

Three blocks northwest of Plaza San Martín is one of the city's most delightful museums, the **Museo de Arte Hispanoamericano Isaac Fernández Blanco** ⓘ *Suipacha 1422, www.museofernandezblanco.buenosaires.gob.ar, Tue-Fri, 1400-1900, Sat and Sun 1100-1900, US$0.30, Thu free, closed Jan, for guided visits in English or French, T011-4327 0228, guided tours in Spanish Sat, Sun 1600*. Housed in a beautiful 1920s neo-colonial mansion with tiled Spanish-style gardens, it contains a fascinating collection of colonial art, with fine Cuzqueño school paintings, and dazzling ornate silverware from Alto Perú and Río de la Plata. There are also temporary exhibitions of Latin American art. Highly recommended.

North of Plaza San Martín is **Retiro railway station**, really three separate terminals. The area is not safe to walk around, but if you're catching a train, drop in to see the oldest and finest of these, the **Mitre**, dating from 1908, a classical construction with an atmospheric interior, and a fantastic refurbished 1900s *confitería* with the original bar and high wooden ceilings – a great place for a coffee. Behind the station is the **Museo Nacional Ferroviario** ⓘ *accessed from Av del Libertador 405, T011-4318 3343, Mon-Fri 1030-1600, free*, which contains locomotives, machinery and documents on the history of Argentine railways.

Avenida 9 de Julio is the world's widest thoroughfare, with nine lanes of traffic in each direction, leading south to Plaza de la Constitución and routes south of the city. It's crossed by the major streets of Avenida de Mayo and Córdoba, and at the junction with Corrientes is the city's famous landmark, a 67-m-tall **obelisk** constructed in 1936, commemorating the 400th anniversary of the city's founding, where football fans traditionally congregate in crowds to celebrate a victory. The city's main shopping street Avenida Santa Fe starts at Plaza San Martín and crosses Avenida 9 de Julio before heading through Retiro and Recoleta to Palermo. It's a huge stretch of shops, but the most well known brands are to be found between Talcahuano and Avenida Pueyrredon.

Four blocks west of the obelisk, you can see art exhibitions, go to the theatre and learn tango at the **Centro Cultural General San Martín** ① *Av Corrientes 1530, www.ccgsm. gov.ar, www.ccgsh.gov.ar, museum US$0.80, Wed free*. It's a rather austere 1970s concrete building, but it houses good photography exhibitions, the Teatro Municipal San Martín (www.teatrosanmartin.com.ar) and a salon of the Museo Municipal de Arte Moderno. There's also a tango information desk at the entrance.

Teatro Colón

① *Main entrance on Libertad, between Tucumán and Viamonte, T011-4378 7132, T011-4378 7133, www.teatrocolon.org.ar. The theatre is over 100 years old and has recently reopened after a multi-million dollar overhaul, just in time for the country's bicentennial in 2010. If you have time, try to see a performance or contact the theatre to do a backstage tour, prices and times not released at time of printing.*

On Avenida 9 de Julio, a block north of the obelisk, Teatro Colón is one of the world's greatest opera houses and one of the city's finest buildings. It opened in 1908 and is an extraordinary testimony to the country's former wealth. Behind the classical façade, the opulent foyer is decorated with three kinds of marble brought from Europe, a Parisian stained glass dome in the roof, and a Venetian-tiled mosaic floor. The perfectly preserved auditorium is French baroque style, from the chandelier in the ceiling (which conceals a chamber where singers or musicians can be hidden to produce music from the heavens) to the French gilded lights and red velvet curtains. It has an almost perfect acoustic, due to the horseshoe shape and the mix of marble and soft fabrics, and an immense stage, 35 m deep. Workshops and rehearsal spaces lie underneath the Avenida 9 de Julio itself, and there are stores of costumes, including 22,000 pairs of shoes.

Puerto Madero

East of the city centre at Puerto Madero, the 19th-century docks have been successfully transformed into an attractive area with lots of good restaurants, cafés, bars and upmarket hotels among the modern developments of offices, shops, housing and even a university campus. It's a good place for a walk, among the tall brick buildings and along the docks, with their cranes and winches now freshly painted. Restaurants are mostly found along the waterside of the old warehouses lining Avenida Alicia M de Justo from the northern end of Dique 4, where you'll find a helpful **tourist information** kiosk in a glass construction under one of the cranes.

Walking south, there are a couple of interesting ships to look at. By Dique 3, there's the **Fragata Presidente Sarmiento** ① *Av Dávila and Perón, T011-4334 9386, daily 0900-2000, US$1, free for children under 5*, which was the Argentine flagship from 1899 to 1938, and is now a museum. Walking further south, in Dique 1, Avenida Juan de Garay, is the **Corbeta Uruguay**, the sailing ship that rescued Otto Nordenskjold's Antarctic expedition in 1903. Also over Dique 3 is the striking harp-like bridge, the **Puente de la Mujer** (Bridge of Women), suspended by cables from a single arm.

Costanera Sur

Buenos Aires has an extraordinary green space right at the heart of the city and on the waterfront. At the southernmost end of Dique 1, cross the pivoting bridge (level with Brazil Street) to the broad avenue of the Costanera Sur. This pleasant wide avenue used to run east of the docks, a fashionable promenade by the waterside in the early 20th century. Now it's separated from the river by the wide splay of land created in a 1970s landfill project, now enjoying a revival, with many restaurants open along the boulevard at night, and it's a pleasant place to walk by day. There's a wonderfully sensuous marble fountain designed by famous Tucumán sculptress Lola Mora, **Las Nereidas**, at the southernmost entrance to the **Reserva Ecológica** ① *entrances at Av Tristán Achával Rodríguez 1550 (take Estados Unidos east from San Telmo), T011-4315 1320, for pedestrians and bikes only, Tue-Sun 0800-1800, in summer closes at 1900, free, bus No 2 passes next to the southern entrance*, where there are more than 200 species of birds, including the curve-billed reed hunter. Free guided tours are available at weekends, 1030 and 1530 (daily in summer), from the administration next to the southern entrance, but much can be seen from the road before then (binoculars useful). Also free nocturnal visits every month on the Friday closest to the full moon (book Monday before, T011-4893 1588). It is a 30-minute walk from the entrance to the river shore, taking about three hours to walk the whole perimeter. In summer it is very hot with little shade. For details (birdwatching, in particular) contact **Aves Argentinas/AOP** (see Tourist information, page).

Recoleta

The area of Recoleta is known as Barrio Norte, the chic place to live in the centre of the capital. Stretching west from Plaza San Martín, beyond Avenida 9 de Julio, Recoleta became a fashionable residential area when wealthy families started to move here from the crowded city centre after a yellow fever outbreak in 1871. Many of its French-style mansions date from the turn of the 20th century, and there are smart apartment blocks with marble entrances in leafy streets, making for a pleasant stroll around the many cafés, art galleries and museums. At its heart is the **Plaza de la Recoleta** by the **Recoleta Cemetery**. Running down its southeastern side is Ortiz, lined with cafés and *confiterías* ranging from the refined and traditional to touristy eateries, most with tables outside. Overhead are the branches of the **gran gomero**, a rubber tree, whose limbs are supported on crutches. At weekends, the **Plaza Francia** is filled with an art and craft market from 1100 until 1800, when the whole place is lively, with street artists and performers.

Recoleta is famous for its cemetery, where Eva Perón is buried, along with other illustrious figures from Argentina's history. **Cementerio de la Recoleta** ① *entrance at Junín 1790, www.cementeriorecoleta.com.ar, not far from Museo de Bellas Artes (see below), T011-4804 7040, www.mnba.org.ar, Tue-Fri 1230-2030, Sat and Sun 0930-2030*, is like a miniature city, its narrow streets weaving between imposing family mausoleums built in every imaginable architectural style, a vast congregation of stone angels on their roofs. To negotiate this enormous labyrinth, a guided tour is recommended, but at the very least you'll want to see Evita Perón's tomb, lying in the Duarte family mausoleum. To find it from the entrance, walk straight ahead to the first tree-filled plaza, turn left, and where this avenue meets a main avenue (go just beyond the Turriata tomb), turn right and then take the third passage on the left.

The former Jesuit church of **El Pilar**, next to the cemetery, is a beautiful example of colonial architecture dating from 1732, restored in 1930. There are stunning 18th-century gold altarpieces made in Alto Peru, and a fine wooden image of San Pedro de Alcántara, attributed to the famous 17th-century Spanish sculptor Alonso Cano, preserved in a side chapel on the left. Downstairs is an interesting small museum of religious art, from whose windows you have a good view of the cemetery next door.

The **Centro Cultural Recoleta** ① *Junín 1930, www.centroculturalrecoleta.org, Tue-Fri 1400-2100, Sat, Sun, holidays 1000-2100, T011-4803 0358*, alongside the Recoleta cemetery, occupying the cloisters of a former monastery, has constantly changing exhibitions of contemporary local art by young artists. Next door, the **Buenos Aires Design Centre** ① *www.designrecoleta.com.ar*, has stylish homewares by contemporary Argentine designers. There are also lots of good restaurants here, some with views over the nearby plazas from their open terraces, recommended for an evening drink at sunset. In **Plaza San Martín de Tours** next door, there are more huge gomera trees with their

4 Recoleta

200 metres
200 yards

Sleeping 🛏
Alvear Palace 1
Art Hotel 4
Four Seasons 3
Palacio Duhau-Park Hyatt 2
Trip Recoleta 5

Eating 🍴
Café Victoria 7
Clásica y Moderna 1
Como en Casa 2
El Sanjuanino 8
La Madeleine 11
Lola 12
Rodi Bar 13
Sirop 14

Tandoor 3

Bars & clubs 🍸
Buller Brewing Company 6
Casa Bar 4
El Living 5
Milion 15
Shamrock 9

extraordinary sinuous roots, and here you're likely to spot one of Buenos Aires' legendary dog walkers, managing an unfeasible 20 or so dogs without tangling their leads. There's a **tourist information booth** ① *T011-4804 5667*, at Ayacuco 1958. **Village Recoleta** ① *T011-4805 2220*, on Vicente López and Junín, houses a multiplex cinema, with a fantastic bookshop and cafés at its entrance.

Recoleta museums

Most of the city's great museums are collected together in Recoleta, where the wide and fast avenue **Avenida del Libertador** runs north from Recoleta towards Palermo, past further parks and squares as well as several major museums. Of these the undoubted star is **Museo de Arte Latinoamericano de Buenos Aires** (MALBA) ① *Av Figueroa Alcorta 3415, T011-4808 6500, www.malba.org.ar, Wed-Mon 1200-2000 (Wed free till 2100), US$1.30, free for ISIC holders, cinema tickets US$4, book in advance*, opened in 2001 to house a permanent collection of Latin American art, and temporary exhibitions. The minimalist building may strike you as rather stark, but the works inside are full of passion – powerful, humorous and moving pieces, very accessible and highly recommended. There's also an elegant café serving delicious food and cakes, and a cinema showing well-chosen art house films, as well as Argentine classics. If you've time for only one museum, make it this one.

For a taste of older Argentine art, visit the **Museo de Bellas Artes** ① *Av del Libertador 1473, T011-4803 0802, www.mnba.org.ar, Tue-Fri 1230-1930, Sat-Sun 0930-1930, guided tours Tue-Sun 1600, 1700, 1800, tours for children in summer Tue-Fri 1100, 1700, Sat-Sun 1700, free*. There's a fairly ordinary survey of European works, but some particularly good post-Impressionist paintings and fine Rodin sculptures. Best of all though, there is a varied collection of Argentine 19th- and 20th-century paintings, sculpture and wooden carvings.

The **Biblioteca Nacional** (National Library) ① *Av del Libertador 1600 and Agüero 2502, T011-4806 6155, www.bn.gov.ar, Mon-Fri 0900-2100, Sat and Sun 1200-1900, closed Jan, excellent guided tours (Spanish) daily 1600 from main entrance, for tours in other languages contact in advance*, is a huge cube standing on four sturdy legs in an attractive garden with a bust of Eva Perón. Only a fraction of its stock of about 1.8 million volumes and 10,000 manuscripts is available, but it's open to visitors, and worth a look to enjoy one of the frequent exhibitions and recitals.

The fabulous **Museo Nacional de Arte Decorativo** ① *Av del Libertador 1902, www.mnad.org.ar, daily 1400-1900, T011-4802 6606, US$0.90, ½-price to ISIC holders, guided tours Wed, Thu, Fri 1630*, is housed in a fabulously elegant building and contains collections of painting, furniture, porcelain, crystal and sculpture. It also hosts classical music concerts on Wednesdays and Thursdays. The French style mansion is worth seeing on it's own, and there is a lovely café outside in the garden.

Offering a real insight into the Argentine soul, the **Museo de Arte Popular José Hernández** ① *Av Libertador 2373, T011-4802 7294, Wed-Sun 1300-1900, US$0.50, free Sun, closed in Feb*, is named after the writer of Argentina's famous epic poem *Martín Fierro*, and contains one of the most complete collections of folkloric art in the country. There are plenty of gaucho artefacts: ornate silver *mates*, wonderful plaited leather *talebartería* and decorated silver stirrups, together with pre-Hispanic artefacts, and paintings from the Cuzco school. There is also a handicrafts shop and library.

Palermo

Palermo is Buenos Aires' most colourful area, growing in recent years from a peaceful residential *barrio* to a seriously hip and chic place to eat, shop and party.

Palermo parks

Palermo was originally named after Giovanni Domenico Palermo who transformed these lands into productive orchards and vineyards in the 17th century. President De Rosas built a sumptuous mansion, **La Quinta**, here in the early 19th century, and Palermo's great parks were established by Sarmiento and designed by Argentina's most famous landscape designer, Charles Thays, in the early 20th century. It remains a sought-after residential area for middle-class *Porteños*, and the wonderful parks are the most popular inner-city green space at weekends. Best not to go at night as they turn into an unofficial 'red-light' district.

Of this series of parks, the **Parque Tres de Febrero** ① *Mon-Fri 0800-1800, Sat and Sun 0800-2000 in winter, daily 0800-2000*, is the largest, with lakes and a really beautiful rose garden, especially in spring time when the displays are particularly abundant and fragrant. Also in the park is the **Museo de Arte Moderno Eduardo Sivori** ① *T011- 4774 9452, www.museosivori.org.ar, Tue-Fri 1200-2000 (winter 1800), Sat and Sun 1000-2000 (winter 1800), US$0.60, Sat and Wed free*, where you can immerse yourself in a fine collection of Argentine art, with 19th- and 20th-century paintings, engravings, tapestries and sculptures. South of here is the beautifully harmonious **Japanese garden** ① *T011- 4804 4922, www.jardinjapones.org.ar, daily 1000-1800, US$1.50, guided visits Sat 1500, 1600*, with huge koi to feed, and little bridges over ornate streams, a charming place to walk and delightful for children. There's also a good café with Japanese dishes available among the usual menu, and also the **Japanese-Argentine Cultural Centre** where you can learn flower arranging, tea ceremony and origami. To the east of both of these is the wonderful alien spaceship-like building of the **planetarium** ① *T011-4771 9393, www.planetario.gov.ar, museum Mon-Fri 1000-1500, free, fantastic planetarium shows (in Spanish), US$2.50*, with several impressive meteorites from Campo del Cielo at its entrance. The **Jardín Zoológico, Las Heras and Sarmiento** ① *T011-4011 9900, www.zoobuenos aires.com.ar, daily 1000-1900, guided visits available, US$6, children under 13 free*, west of the Japanese gardens, has a decent collection of animals, in spacious surroundings, and an even more impressive collection of buildings of all kinds of styles, in grounds landscaped by Charles Thays. The llamas and guanacos are particularly appealing, especially if you don't get to see them in their native habitats elsewhere in the country.

The **Municipal Botanical Gardens** ① *west of the zoo at Santa Fe 2951, daily 0800-1800, free*, form one of the most appealing parts of the parks, despite being a little unkempt. Thays designed the gardens in 1902, and its different areas represent various regions of Argentina with characteristic specimens; particularly interesting are the trees native to the different provinces. North of the zoo are the showgrounds of the **Sociedad Rural Argentina** ① *entrance is from Plaza Italia (take Subte, line D)*, where the Annual Livestock Exhibition, known as Exposición Rural, is staged in July/August, providing interesting insights into Argentine society, not to mention truck loads of livestock, horses and roosters on display.

Further north is the 45,000-seater Palermo race track, **Hipódromo Argentino** ① *T011-4777 9001, www.palermo.com.ar*, where races are held on average 10 days per

5 Palermo

Las Cañitas

Buenos Aires maps
1 Buenos Aires orientation, page 27
2 Metro (Subte), page 28
3 Buenos Aires centre, page 32
4 Recoleta, page 38
5 Palermo, page 41
6 San Telmo, page 44

Sleeping
Bait 15
Bo Bo 4
Casa Alfaro 6
Casa Esmeralda 14
Che Lulu 5
Costa Rica 12
Cypress In 7
Five Cool Rooms 3
Glu 17
Home 8
Hostel Suites Palermo 18
Krista 9

Legado Mítico 11
Malabia House 1
Solar Soler 10
Tango Backpackers Hostel 2
Vida Baires 16
Zentrum Boutique Hostel 13

Eating
Baez 9
Bar 6 30
Bio 14
B-Blue 5
Cabernet 18

Campo Bravo 12
Cluny 31
De la Ostia 10
Dominga 20
Eh! Santino 15
El Diamante 21
El Manto 22
El Preferido de Palermo 13
Eterna Cadencia 23
Garum 24
Janio 25
Krishna 1
La Cabrera 2

Mark's Deli 26
Miranda 27
Morelia 8
Novecento 11
Olsen 3
Omm 28
Omm Carnes 29
Persicco 17
Social Paraíso 7
Un' Altra Volta 4

month; it's well worth a visit even for non-racegoers. Nearby are the **Municipal Golf Club**, **Buenos Aires Lawn Tennis Club**, riding clubs and polo field, and the **Club de Gimnasia y Esgrima** (Athletic and Fencing Club). The parks are bordered to the north by Aeroparque (Jorge Newbery Airport), the city's domestic airport.

Palermo Viejo

The most atmospheric, and oldest, part of Palermo can be found in the quadrant between the Córdoba and Santa Fe, south of Juan B Justo and north of Avenida Scalabrini Ortiz. This area is also known as **Palermo Soho** (the two names are interchangeable), supposedly because of similarities with SoHo in New York, rather than London. You'll also hear people mention **Palermo Hollywood**, which is on the other side of the railway tracks and Avenida Juan B Justo which bisects the area. There are fewer shops in this part, and it's so-called because of the number of TV and film companies based here, but there are lots of restaurants and bars, so it's worth exploring. The whole of Palermo is a very seductive place, with its cobbled streets lined with trees, tall bohemian houses bedecked with flowers and plants, and leafy plazas. It's become a very fashionable place to live, but it's even more popular among young *Porteños* shopping for contemporary clothing and interiors, and drinking in chic bars in the evenings. There's no *Subte* station in the middle of Palermo, but there are three stations within five blocks or so, along Avenida Santa Fe, and there are buses which pass close by. A taxi from San Telmo to Palermo costs about US$8.

To start exploring, take the *Subte* (Line D) to either Scalabrini Ortiz, Plaza Italia or Palermo stations (depending on where you want to start). Walk up towards **Plaza Palermo Viejo** also called **Plaza Armenia** or to Plaza Serrano officially called **Plaza Cortázar**, named after Argentina's famous novelist and writer, whose novel *Rayuela* (Hopscotch) is set around here. These two plazas are both surrounded by cafés and bars, and in the four blocks between are all the clothing and accessories shops you could ever need (see Shopping, page 62, for more details). Meander up **Malabia**, and then around streets **Costa Rica**, **El Salvador** and **Honduras**, with detours along Armenia and Guruchaga when some boutique catches your eye. For a list of recommended clothes shops, see page 64. Even if you loathe shopping, Palermo Viejo will appeal since the whole area is wide open and relaxed, and it retains the quiet atmosphere of a residential district.

For bars and restaurants, you can wander further afield and stray onto the other side of Juan B Justo, though note that you can only cross the railway tracks at Honduras, Paraguay and Santa Fe. Alternatively, take a Radio Taxi from the centre of town straight to one of the restaurants recommended in this guide, and wander the nearby blocks to lap up the atmosphere and satisfy yourself there's nowhere you fancy more. So many new restaurants have opened up in the last few years that you'll be spoilt for choice. Palermo is a great place for meeting in the evenings, with bars and restaurants attracting lively crowds of trendy locals as well as increasing numbers of tourists. On the northwestern edge of Palermo, separated from the main area by yet another railway line, is **Las Cañitas**, a hugely popular area of restaurants centred around **Báez**.

South of the centre

San Telmo

The city's most atmospheric *barrio* is also its oldest. San Telmo starts south of the Plaza de Mayo, and is built along a slope which was once the old beach of the Río de la Plata. Formerly one of the wealthiest areas of the city, it was abandoned by the rich during a serious outbreak of yellow fever in 1871, and so was never modernized or destroyed for rebuilding like much of the rest of the city. San Telmo is one of the few areas where buildings have survived from the mid-19th century, crumbling and largely unchanged, so it's a delightful place to stroll and explore the artists' studios and small museums hidden away in its narrow streets, with plenty of cafés and shops selling antiques, records, handmade shoes, second-hand books and crafts of all kinds. In the last couple of years, new boutiques, design shops and chic bars (and hotels) have been opening up in newly renovated old houses in San Telmo and moving out towards Montserrat too, similar to those in Palermo Viejo.

A quiet place to meander during the week, the *barrio* comes alive on Sundays when there's an antiques and bric-a-brac market held in the central **Plaza Dorrego**, a small square enclosed by charming old houses. This is a good place to start exploring, after enjoying the free tango demonstrations that take place near the plaza on Sundays 1000-1800, and sometimes during the week as well. Behind the plaza, on Carlos Calvo (entrances on Bolívar, Estados Unidos and Defensa too), there's a wonderful indoor fruit market – **Mercado de San Telmo** built in 1897, which also has some antiques and vintage clothes. Walk south along Defensa, filled with street musicians on Sundays, many of them excellent, and pop into the artists' studios, antique shops and cafés that line the street. Just a block from the plaza is the white stuccoed church of **San Pedro González Telmo** ① *Humerto Primero, T011-4361 1168, Mon-Sat 0830-1200, 16-1900, guided tours Sun at 1500, 1600, free.* Begun by the Jesuits in 1734, but only finished in 1931, it's a wonderful confection of styles with ornate baroque columns and Spanish-style tiles.

One block further south, in an old tobacco warehouse, the **Museo de Arte Moderno de Buenos Aires** ① *San Juan 350, T011-4361 1121, www.museos.buenosaires.gov.ar/mam.htm, which is currently closed for renovations*, houses good visiting exhibitions of contemporary international and Argentine art. Due to re-open in 2011.

At the end of Defensa is **Parque Lezama** ① *Defensa and Brasil, Sat and Sun 1000-2000*, originally one of the most beautiful parks in the city, but now a little run down, and not a safe place to wander at night. According to tradition, Pedro de Mendoza founded the city on this spot in 1535, and there's an imposing statue to him in the centre of the park. Also on this corner you'll find the famous **Bar Británico** which has been open almost continuously since 1960. It has featured in films (including *The Motorcycle Diaries*) and was an institution in the suburb, but has been refurbished by new owners. It is still open 24 hours and is a good place to have a coffee and watch the world go by. On the west side of the park is the **Museo Histórico Nacional** ① *Defensa 1600, T011-4307 1182, Wed-Sun 1100-1800, US$0.50, guided tours Sat-Sun 1530*, which presents the history of the city and of Argentina through the key historical figures and events, with some impressive artefacts, portraits and war paintings, particularly of San Martín. Unfortunately, there's currently little information available in English.

There is an ever-growing number of restaurants along Defensa, many of them cheap and lively places to eat, and several venues offering tango shows. The best is the historical

El Viejo Almacén ① *Independencia and Balcarce, T011-4307 7388, www.viejoalmacen. com, open daily, dinner from 2000, show 2200, US$70 with all drinks, dinner and show US$105, show only US$58,* started by celebrated tango singer Edmundo Rivero in the late

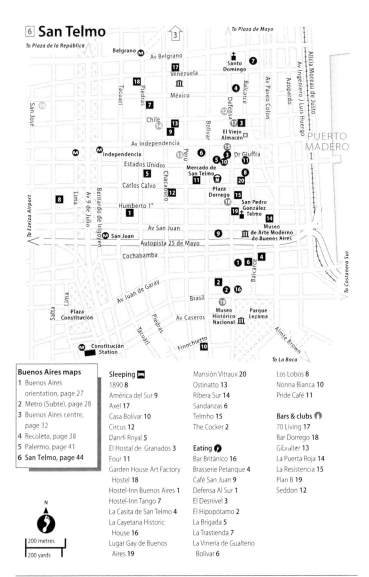

6 San Telmo

Carlos Gardel

To this day there is still a lot of controversy about the origins of Argentina's favourite performer. Most people argue that Gardel, the legendary singer whose name is virtually synonymous with tango, was born in 1890 in Toulouse, France, to Berthe Gardés and an unknown father. To avoid social stigma, his mother decided to emigrate to the Abasto market area of Buenos Aires when her son was just two years old, and it was partly these humble beginnings that helped him to become an icon for poor *Porteños*.

Just as the exact origin of tango itself is something of a mystery, Gardel's formative years around the city are obscure, until around 1912 when he began his artistic career in earnest, performing as one half of the duo Gardel-Razzano. He began his recording career with Columbia with a recording of 15 traditional songs, but it was with his rendition of *Mi Noche Triste* (My Sorrowful Night) in 1917, that his mellifluous voice became known. *Astango-canción* became

popular – the song rather than just a musical accompaniment to the dance – Gardel's career took off, and by the early 1920s he was singing entirely within this new genre, and achieving success as far afield as Madrid.

Gardel became a solo artist in 1925 and with his charm and natural machismo was the very epitome of tango both in Argentina and, following his tours to Europe, around the world. Between 1933 and 1935, he was based in New York, starring in numerous Spanish-speaking films, and the English language *The Tango on Broadway* in 1934. On 24 June 1935, while on a tour of South America, his plane from Bogotá to Cali crashed into another on the ground while taking off. Gardel was killed instantly, he was only 45. Gardel had recorded some 900 songs during his relatively short career, and the brilliance of his voice, the way he represented the spirit of the Río de la Plata to his fans at home, and the untimely nature of his dramatic death ensured the endurance of his popularity.

1960s. Here the city's finest tango dancers demonstrate their extraordinary skills in a small, atmospheric theatre, with excellent live music and singing from some of the great names of tango. Highly recommended. There are plenty of good restaurants sprinkled through San Telmo, and lots of hostels are here too.

La Boca

East of the Plaza de Mayo, behind the Casa Rosada, a broad avenue, Paseo Colón, runs south towards the old port district of La Boca, where the polluted Riachuelo river flows into the Plata. An area of heavy Italian immigration in the early 1900s, La Boca is known for the brightly painted blue, yellow and lime green zinc façades of its houses, a tradition brought over by Genoese immigrants who painted their homes with the leftover paint from ships. It's a much-touted tourist destination, but very disappointing in reality. There is nothing authentic left of the area, and just one block of brightly painted houses to see on pedestrianized **El Caminito**, put there, somewhat cynically, by the Buenos Aires tourist board. El Caminito leads west from the little triangular plaza **La Vuelta de Rocha**, and this street is in fact the only place you're allowed to visit in La Boca, since policemen are permanently stationed there to stop tourists from straying further. This is because the area is apparently rife with petty crime and tourist muggings are a common occurrence. There's a small arcade of artists' workshops and a couple of cafés in the **Centro Cultural de los Artistas**, with tango dancers, street entertainers and touristy souvenir shops. You might be tempted to stray from this touristy area and find the 'real' La Boca: don't. The surrounding streets are notorious for crime, you will almost certainly be a very obvious target, and in any case, the Riachuelo river is far from picturesque, with its distinctive rotting smell. To reach La Boca from the centre, phone for a Radio Taxi, US$5 from downtown (see Ins and outs, page 6) and call from the *locutorio* in Centro Cultural for a taxi to take you home. Police are on hand in the Vuelta de Rocha to help and advise tourists. There is a freephone number to contact the **tourist police office** ① *T0800-999 5000, staff speak English and other European languages.*

The real attractions here are two fine museums: La Boca really owes its fame to the artist Benito Quinquela Martín (1890-1977) who painted its ships, docks and workers all his life, and whose vivid and colourful paintings can be seen in the **Museo de Bellas Artes Benito Quinquela** ① *Pedro de Mendoza 1835, T011-4301 1080, Tue-Sun 1030-1730, closed Jan, US$0.40.* The artist lived here for many years, and you can also see his own extensive collection of paintings by Argentine artists, and sculpture on a roof terrace with wonderful views over the whole port, revealing the marginalized poverty behind the coloured zinc façades. There's more contemporary art a block away in the **Fundacíon Proa** ① *Av Pedro de Mendoza 1929, T011-4104 1000, www.proa.org, Tue-Sun 1100-1900, guided visits Tue-Fri 1700, Sat and Sun 1500 and 1700, US$1.50,* a modern space opened in 1996 behind the ornate Italianate façade of a 1908 warehouse, showing temporary exhibitions of Argentine, Latin American and international contemporary art. Check the press for details. The roof terrace here is also great, and a nightclub venue.

La Boca is home to one of the country's great football teams, **Boca Juniors** (see page 66), and the area is especially rowdy when they're playing at home. Football is one of the great Argentine experiences, and the easiest way to go to a match is as part of a group arranged with a company such as **Tangol** (see Tour operators, page 68). Aficionados of the beautiful game will be entertained by the **Museo de la Pasión Boquense** ① *Brandsen 805, T011-4362 1100, daily 1000-1800 (times change if a match is on).* US$6.50, or US$9 for museum entry and a stadium tour (yes, you'll see Maradona's personal box).

Buenos Aires listings

For Sleeping and Eating price codes and other relevant information, see pages 11 17.

● Sleeping

In the current economic climate, some hotels are offering discounts for multi-night stays, so it is worth checking out several hotels to get the cheapest deal. The tourist offices at both airports can book hotels, and if you pay in pesos, you can sometimes get further discounts.

City centre and Recoleta *p29, maps p32 and p38*

$$$$ 725 Continental, Av Roque Saenz Peña 725, T011-4131 6000, www.725continental. com. Modern design business hotel in the centre. Wonderful bar, stunning roof-top pool, gym with a view. Very chic.

$$$$ Alvear Palace, Av Alvear 1891, T/F011-4808 2100, www.alvearpalace.com. The height of elegance, an impeccably preserved

1930s Recoleta palace, taking you back in time to Buenos Aires' wealthy heyday. A marble foyer, with Louis XV-style chairs and an orangery where you can take tea with superb patisseries (US$15). Recommended.

$$$$ Casa Calma, Suipacha 1015, T011-5199 2800, www.casacalma.com.ar. Despite its downtown setting this sleek, yet homely luxury boutique hotel has managed to create a relaxing haven with rainforest music in the hallways, a wellness centre and an honesty bar.

$$$$ Four Seasons, Posadas 1086, T011-4321 1200, www.fourseasons.com/buenosaires. A modern palace decorated in traditional style, offering sumptuous luxury in an exclusive atmosphere. Spacious public areas, adorned with paintings and flowers, chic, lavishly decorated rooms, and 7 suites in **La Mansión** where Madonna filmed *Evita* and numerous famous guests have enjoyed the residence, pool and health club.

$$$$ Marriott Plaza, Florida 1005, T011-4318 3000, www.marriottplaza.com.ar. With a superb location overlooking Plaza San Martín, this is the city's most historic hotel, built in Parisian style in 1909, and retaining period elegance in the public rooms and bedrooms, which are charming and luxurious. A pool and fitness centre, excellent restaurant, the **Plaza Grill**, and very good service throughout.

$$$$ Palacio Duhau-Park Hyatt, Av Alvear 1661, T011-51711234, www.buenosaires. park.hyatt.com. Refurbished aristocratic mansion in the heart of Recoleta, with wonderful gardens and a great terrace for enjoying an evening cocktail.

$$$$ Panamericano, Carlos Pellegrini 551, T011-4348 5000, www.panamericano news.com. Smart and modern city hotel, with luxurious and tasteful rooms, a lovely covered rooftop pool with a million dollar view of Av 9 de Julio, and superb restaurant, **Tomo 1**. Excellent service too.

$$$ Art Hotel, Azcuénaga 1268, T011-4821 4744, www.arthotel.com.ar. Great location on a quiet street in Recoleta and handy for the *Subte* and shopping in Santa Fe, this is a reliable and comfortable little hotel with small, neat, well-equipped rooms, and good breakfasts. It's a pricey option but made worthwhile by the great service from all the multilingual staff who go out of their way to make your stay comfortable. Free internet. Recommended.

$$$ Bisonte Palace, Marcelo T de Alvear 902, T011-43284751, www.hotelesbisonte.com. A delightful old place, with calm entrance foyer, which remains gracious thanks to charming and courteous staff. The rooms are modern and spacious, breakfast is ample, and it is in a good location.

$$$ Castelar, Av de Mayo 1152, T011- 4383 5000, www.castelarhotel.com.ar. Wonderfully elegant 1920s hotel which retains all the original features in the grand entrance and bar. Cosy bedrooms (some a bit too cosy), helpful staff, and excellent value. Ask if there's going to be a party, though, as it can be very noisy. Also a spa with Turkish baths and massage. Recommended.

$$$ Dolmen, Suipacha 1079, T011-4315 7117, www.hoteldolmen.com.ar. In a good location, this hotel has a spacious entrance lobby, with a calm relaxing atmosphere, good professional service, comfortable modern well-designed rooms, and a little pool.

$$$ La Cayetana Historic House, México 1330, T011-43832230, www.lacayetana hotel.com.ar. This fabulous 1820s restored house has 11 suites set off a lovely courtyard. Each room is individually designed, there is Wi-Fi, buffet breakfast and parking. Located a little out of the centre in the quiet suburb of Monserrat. Recommended.

$$$ Moreno, 376 Moreno, T011-6091 2000, www.morenobuenosaires.com. Decorated in dark, rich tones this hotel is the best value in its category. Large rooms, some with a view over the nearby basilica, and only 150 m to Plaza de Mayo. Jacuzzi, gym and chic bar. Recommended.

$$$ NH City Hotel, Bolívar 160, T011-4121 6464, www.nh-hoteles.com. Very chic, with perfect minimalist design for a discerning younger clientele, this is one of 8 in the Spanish-owned chain in central Buenos Aires (see the website for the others), with beautifully designed modern interiors in a 1930s building off Plaza de Mayo, and luxurious rooms. Small rooftop pool, good restaurant.

$$$ Plaza San Martín Suites, Suipacha 1092, T011-43284740, www.plazasan martin.com.ar. Neat modern self-contained apartments, comfortable and attractively decorated, with lounge and little kitchen, so that you can relax in privacy, right in the city centre, with all the services of a hotel. Sauna, gym, room service. Good value.

$$$ Waldorf, Paraguay 450, T011-312 2071, www.waldorf-hotel.com.ar. Welcoming staff and a comfortable mixture of traditional and modern in this centrally located hotel. Good value, with a buffet breakfast, English spoken. Recommended.

$$ Frossard, Tucumán 686, T011-4322 1811, www.hotelfrossard.com.ar. A lovely old 1940s building with high ceilings and the original doors, attractively modernized, and though the rooms are small, the staff are welcoming. This is good value and near Florida.

$$ Goya, Suipacha 748, T011-4322 9269, www.goyahotel.com.ar. A range of rooms offered in this friendly, welcoming and central place, worth paying for the superior rooms (**$$$**), though all are comfortable and well maintained. Good breakfast, English spoken.

$$ Hispano, Av De Mayo 861, T011-4345 2020, www.hhispano.com.ar. This hotel has been welcoming budget travellers since the 1950s. Rooms are plain but comfortable, set around a light courtyard, with a section of garden to enjoy. Only 3 blocks from the Casa Rosada, and 2 from the busy pedestrianized Florida.

$$ Marbella, Av de Mayo 1261, T/F011-4383 3573, www.hotelmarbella.com.ar. Modernized and central, though quiet. Breakfast included, English, French, Italian, Portuguese and German spoken. Highly recommended.

$$ The Clan House, Alsina 817, T011-4331 4448, www.bedandbreakfastclan.com.ar. This wonderful B&B has 17 brightly coloured, modern rooms, and offers buffet breakfast, Wi-Fi and a small but lovely terrace. Recommended.

$ O'Rei, Lavalle 733, T011-4393 7186, www.hotelorei.com.ar. Slightly cheaper without bath, central, simple but comfortable, spotless, laundry facilities, helpful staff.

Hostels

$ pp 06Central, Maipú 306, T011-5219 0052, www.06centralhostel.com. A few metres from the Obelisco and the theatre street of Corrientes, this hostel offers simple, clean, spacious dorms, and nicely decorated doubles (**$$**). Kitchen, cosy communal area.

$ pp About Baires Hostel, Viamonte 982, T011-4328 4616, www.aboutbaireshostel. com. Located in a lovely building, this hostel is only a short walk to the centre, shopping street Av Santa Fe and the Obelisco. Same-sex dorms are available (**$**), as are double rooms (**$$**). Prices include breakfast.

$ pp BA Stop, Rivadavia 1194, T011-4382 7406, www.bastop.com. Set in a converted 1900s corner block, the walls are covered in fun murals, and the communal areas are inviting. Pool table and buffet breakfast. May be a little noisy as it is right in the middle of the city.

$ Hostel Downtown, Callao 341, San Nicolás, T011-4372 8898, www.laroccahostel.com. English-speaking staff, breakfast included and free Wi-Fi.

$ pp Hostel Suites Obelisco, Av Corrientes 830, T011-4328 4040, www.hostelsuites. com. Top-notch hostel, with bright new furnishings and friendly staff. Great facilities, tourist info desk and lots of organized activities. They will organize a free transfer from Ezeiza international airport if you book more than 1 night. Dorms and doubles (**$$**) available. HI discount.

$ pp **Lime House**, Lima 11, T011-4383 4561, www.limehouse.com.ar. Fun, lively hostel that organizes bar nights and has a residents-only bar in the reception. Located on busy 9 de Julio so some rooms may be noisy especially those close to the reception/bar and pool table, but the staff and the welcoming atmosphere makes this a fun place to stay. Doubles (**$**) available.

$ pp **Milhouse Hostel**, H Yrigoyen 959, T011-4383 9383, www.milhousehostel.com. This hostel, set in a fantastic 1890 building, is for travellers who want to make friends and party. It's lots of fun and very lively so be prepared. Tours can be booked from the reception.

$ pp **Portal del Sur**, Hipólito Yrigoyen 855, T011-4342 2821, www.portaldelsurba.com.ar. Nice dorms, and especially lovely double (**$$**) and single rooms available. Converted 19th-century building, with 4 storeys of private rooms. Recommended for single travellers.

$ pp **Trip Recoleta**, Vincente López 2180, T011-4807 8726, www.triprecoleta.com.ar. New, spotless dorms and doubles (**$$**) decorated in a chic modern style, right next to the Recoleta cemetery and many popular bars and cafés. Wi-Fi and nice terrace.

$ pp **V&S**, Viamonte 887, T011-4322 0994, www.hostelclub.com. Attractive double rooms with bath (**$$**). This is one of the city's best-loved hostels, central and beautifully run by friendly English-speaking staff, there's a welcoming little café and place to sit, a tiny kitchen, internet access and lots of tours arranged, plus tango nights, etc. Good place to meet people. Highly recommended.

Puerto Madero *p36*

$$$$ Faena Hotel + Universe, Martha Salotti 445, Dique 2, T011-4010 9000, www.faena hotelanduniverse.com. One of the best hotels in the world, this is where the rich and famous stay. Lush, red drapery fills the lobby and the luxury rooms. Stylish swimming pool, extensive gym and glove-wearing men who open doors for you. If you can't afford to stay here, which is most of us, see a tango show or have a drink in the bar at least.

$$$$ Hilton, Av Macacha Güemes 351, Puerto Madero, T011-4891 0000, www.hilton.com. A modern business hotel built in the revamped docks area with views of the Costanera Sur, and with plenty of restaurants nearby, this has neat functional rooms, the **El Faro** restaurant, a health club and pool.

Palermo *p40, map p41*

$$$$ Bo Bo, Guatemala 4882, Palermo Viejo, T011-4774 0505, www.bobohotel.com. Very chic and one of the most welcoming places to stay in Palermo. Bo Bo has just 7 rooms, designed around different themes, though all are warm, elegant and minimalist, with stylish bathrooms (some with disabled access). There's also an excellent restaurant (**$$**) and bar, relaxing places in the evening, with lots of dark wood and smart tables, serving very classy food. Great service from friendly staff, who all speak English. Recommended.

$$$$ Home, Honduras 5860, T011-4778 1008, www.homebuenosaires.com. Another trendy boutique hotel, this one in Palermo Hollywood, with bold 1950s-inspired textiles and minimalist concrete floors, creating a funky vibrant urban chic feel. Just a handful of minimalist rooms around a bar serving light snacks (soup, salads and tapas). Small pool and space to sunbathe at the back. A good place to hang out in the evenings.

$$$$ Legado Mítico, Gurruchaga 1848, T011- 4833 1300, www.legadomitico.com. •

Stylishly designed small hotel with 11 beautiful rooms all subtly thematic. Named after Argentine cultural legends such as Victoria Ocampo, Ernesto Guevara and Jorge Luis Borges, they use local designs, products and art works. Pure luxury. Highly recommended.

$$$$ The Glu Hotel, Godoy Cruz 1733, T011- 4831 4646, www.thegluhotel.com. Right in the heart of trendy Palermo, a stone's throw from the markets at Plaza Serrano, this hotel is new, modern and recommended. Its huge rooms have all the mod-cons and the roof-top jacuzzi is exactly what you'll need after a long day shopping in the surrounding boutiques.

$$$ Craft Hip Hotel, Nicaragua 4583, T011-4833 0060, www.crafthotel.com. With a running theme of white in its 10 rooms, this hotel is a real find. Right on Plaza Armenia and close to shops, bars and restaurants, the rooms are small but imaginatively done out with flatscreen TVs, ipods, Wi-Fi and there is an extremely welcoming roof-top terrace.

$$$ Cypress In, Costa Rica 4828, Palermo Viejo, T011-4833 5834, www.cypressin.com. This cosy, compact B&B offers 8 neat rooms on 2 floors, decorated in pleasing stark modern style, in a centrally located house, where the staff are very friendly. Stylish, small sitting and dining area, and outside patio. Charming. Very good value. Recommended.

$$$ Five Cool Rooms, Honduras 4742, T011-5235 5555, www.fivebuenosaires.com. Too cool for its own good perhaps, the style here is brutal concrete with lots of black wood in the spacious rooms, all with king-size beds and bathrooms. There's a living room with DVDs to watch and internet. There's a terrace upstairs too. It's a bit over-priced, but the staff are efficient and speak fluent English.

$$$ Hotel Costa Rica, Costa Rica 4137/39, T011-4864 7390, www.hotelcostarica.com.ar. Small boutique hotel, with minimalist design and a bright, welcoming air. Lovely terrace to sunbathe on. 3 blocks from Plaza Palermo Viejo with its restaurants and boutiques.

$$$ Krista, Bonpland 1665, T011-4771 4697, www.kristahotel.com.ar. A delightful surprise: this intimate boutique hotel is hidden behind the plain façade of an elegant townhouse, once owned by Perón's doctor. In Palermo Hollywood, so well-placed for restaurants. It's a very appealing place to stay, and good value with its comfortable, calm, individually designed spacious rooms, all with simple bathrooms and smart bedlinen. Wi-Fi, wheelchair access. A real gem. Recommended.

$$$ Malabia House, Malabia 1555, Palermo Viejo, T011-4833 2410, www.malabiahouse. com.ar. An elegant B&B in a tastefully converted old house, with 15 light and airy individually designed bedrooms in white and pale green, and lovely calm sitting rooms. Great breakfast. This was the original Palermo boutique hotel, and while it's not the cheapest of the options available, and always booked in advance, it's recommended as a reliable and welcoming option.

$$$ Solar Soler, Soler 5676, T011-4776 3065, www.solarsoler.com.ar. Very homely and extremely welcoming B&B in a great location in an old town house in Palermo Hollywood. Recommended for its excellent service and charming multilingual staff. All rooms have bathrooms (ask for the quiet ones at the back), there's free internet and the breakfasts are good. Recommended.

$$$ Vida Baires, Gallo 1483, T011-4827 0750, www.vidabaires.com.ar. Located in the residential section of Palermo, close to shops and public transport, this French-style building has been converted into a lovely boutique hotel with 7 clean, light and attractive rooms. Lovely original features and friendly welcome.

$$ Casa Alfaro, Gurruchaga 2155, T011-4831 0517. Homely rustic style in this converted old house, with exposed brick walls, red stone floors and lots of woven rugs.

A variety of rooms for 2-4, some with bathrooms, and quieter rooms at the back, where there's a lovely little garden. The whole place is clean and neat, and the owner speaks English.

$$ Che Lulu, Emilio Zola 5185, T011-4772 0289, www.chelulu.com. Some double rooms and more hostel-style accommodation (**$**) in this friendly, rambling, laid-back house along a quaint quiet street just a few blocks from Palermo *Subte*. Not luxurious but great value and very welcoming. Often recommended.

Hostels

$ pp Bait, El Salvador 5115, T011-4774 3088, www.baitba.com. Small, friendly and located 3 blocks from the main plaza. Rooms are simply decorated, and there is a small private bar upstairs which serves snacks and cold beer.

$ pp Casa Esmeralda, Honduras 5765, T011-4772 2446, www.casaesmeralda.com.ar. Laid-back, dorms and doubles (**$$**), neat garden with hammocks and fishpond. Sebastián, owner of trendy bars **La Cigale** and **Zanzibar**, offers basic comfort with great charm.

$$ Hostel Palermo, Córdoba 3874, T011-4866 6423, www.laroccavip.com. Breakfast included, free Wi-Fi, rooftop terrace. Singles, doubles and dorms.

$ pp Hostel Suites Palermo, Charcas 4752, T011-4773 0806, www.hostelsuitespalermo. com. Located at the busy end of Palermo, near the zoo, this hostel is warm and welcoming, and is only a short walk to the closet *Subte* stop. Dorms and private rooms (**$$**). HI discount.

$ pp Tango Backpackers Hostel, Paraguay 4601, T011-4776 6871, www.tangobp.com. Well situated to enjoy Palermo's nightlife, this is a friendly hostel with shared rooms and doubles (**$**), all the usual facilities plus its own restaurant. HI discount.

$ pp Zentrum Boutique Hostel, Costa Rica 4520, T011-4833 9518, www.zentrumhostel.

com.ar. More a boutique hotel with some dorm beds, this hostel is located in a renovated townhouse using stylish, modern designs. Double rooms without bathroom (**$$**) and with bathroom (**$$$**) are highly recommended. Enjoy the wonderful wooden terrace to watch the sun go down.

San Telmo *p43, map p44*

$$$$ Axel Hotel, Venezuela 649, T011-4136 9393, www.axelhotels.com. Stunning gay hotel with 5 floors of stylishly designed rooms, each floor with a cosy living area. Rooftop pool and gourmet restaurant top it off. Recommended.

$$$$ Mansion Vitraux, Carlos Calvo 369, T011-4300 6886, www.mansionvitraux.com. A stylish luxury hotel with only 12 well-designed rooms, nightly wine tastings and gourmet food. Small dipping pool.

$$$$ Dandi Royal, Piedras 922, T011-4307 7623, www.hotelmansiondandiroyal.com. Perfectly restored 1900s house with stunningly elegant entrance hall and some beautiful rooms all decorated in the original style, with luxurious bathrooms. Interesting location between San Telmo and Congreso, and the added benefit of tango classes downstairs. Charming welcome from English-speaking staff, small pool and much better value than most of the boutique hotels.

$$$ 1890 Hotel, Salta 1074, T011-4304 8798, www.1890hotel.com.ar. Located just outside San Telmo, this fabulous boutique hotel has 6 rooms all decorated in a modern and attractive way with a/c, heating and wonderful bathrooms. The building itself is a renovated 19th-century house and there is a tranquil patio for relaxing.

$$$ Casa Bolívar, Finochietto 524, T011-4300 3619, www.casabolivar.com. Each room in this wonderful hotel has a different theme, from Oriental, to Pop, to art deco, and they all have a kitchenette and modern bathrooms. Serving breakfast, but no other meals, this is a good longer-term option.

$$$ La Casita de San Telmo, Cochabamba 286 T011-4307 5073, www.lacasitadesan telmo.com. A restored 1840s house, 7 rooms, most of which open onto a garden with a beautiful fig tree. The owners are tango fans. Rooms are rented by the day, week or month.

$$$ Lugar Gay de Buenos Aires, Defensa 1120, T011-4300 4747, www.lugargay.com.ar. A men-only gay B&B with 8 comfortable rooms. There is a video room and jacuzzi, and it is located a stone's throw from Plaza Dorrego.

$$$ Ribera Sur, Paseo Colón 1145, between San Juan and Humberto 1, www.riberasur hotel.com.ar. Slightly strange location on a busy 8-lane road on the limit of San Telmo, but inside, this hotel offers a peaceful oasis in shades of grey and white. Chic rooms, great bar downstairs and a tiny pool.

$$$ Telmho, Defensa 1086, T011-4116 5467, www.telmho-hotel.com.ar. Smartly decorated doubles with huge beds and windows that open up onto the famous Plaza Dorrego. See the market from the wonderful roof garden. Flatscreen TVs, new modern bathrooms and helpful staff.

$$$ The Cocker, Av Garay 458, T011-4362 8451, www.thecocker.com. In the heart of the antiques district, this art nouveau house has been cleverly and tastefully restored. It now offers a perfect urban retreat with stylish suites, a cosy, light living room and delightful roof terraces and gardens. Recommended.

$$$ The Four, Carlos Calvo 535, T011-4362 1729, www.thefourhotel.com. In the heart of San Telmo this 1930s building has been converted into a lovely B&B with 6 rooms named after the years of important events in the neighbourhood. Appealing terrace, as well as welcoming staff. Recommended.

$$ Garden House Art Factory, Piedras 545, T011-4343 1463, www.artfactory ba.com.ar. Watch the sun set from the terrace and bar of this upmarket place. Dorms available (**$**).

Hostels

$ pp América del Sur, Chacabuco 718, T011-4300 5525, www.americahostel.com.ar. Large, newly purpose-built hostel with hotel-like double rooms (**$$$**) and a fantastic terrace. New facilities throughout and a great location.

$ pp Circus, Chacabuco 1020, T011-4878 7786, www.hostelcircus.com. New 'luxury' hostel with clean and stylish rooms, new fittings throughout the tastefully renovated building, and even a small heated swimming pool. Doubles (**$$**) available.

$ pp El Hostal de Granados, Chile 374, T011-4362 5600, www.hostaldegranados. com.ar. Small, well-equipped rooms in an interesting building on a popular street with bars and restaurants, lots of light, for 2 (**$$**) to 4, with bath, breakfast included, kitchen, free internet, laundry service, discounts for longer stays.

$ pp Hostel-Inn Tango, Piedras 680, T011-4300 5764, and **Hostel-Inn Buenos Aires**, Humberto Primero 820, T011-4300 7992, www.hostel-inn.com. Both well-organized hostels in old renovated houses, popular, lively, lots of activities and facilities such as internet, transfers, Spanish lessons. Breakfast included. 20% discount for HI card holders and 10% off long-distance buses.

$ pp Ostinatto, Chile 680, T011-4362 9639, www.ostinatto.com.ar. Converted 5-level 1920s building, which has a huge open-plan kitchen, spacious dorms, a multi-use dance room where Spanish lessons are held and, best of all, a roof terrace where low-costs meals are served. Doubles (**$$**) with or without a bathroom are also available. Located in a quiet but central street. Recommended.

$ pp Sandanzas, Balcarce 1351, T011-4300 7375, www.sandanzas.com.ar. Arty budget hostel run by a group of friends who've created an original and welcoming space, small but with a nice, light, airy feel. Lounge and patio, internet, kitchen, breakfast. Also double rooms (**$**) with own bath.

Apartments/self-catering

If you are staying for more than a few days it will be more cost effective to rent an apartment. That way you can cook your own meals and perhaps share with friends. Apartments cost from US$40 per night, see www.craigslist.com (Argentina pages).

Bahouse, T011-4815 7602, www.bahouse. ar. Very good furnished flats. Well located in Retiro, Recoleta, Belgrano, Palermo and centre.

ByT Argentina, T011-4878 5000, www.byt argentina.com. Accommodation in residences and with host families; also furnished flats.

Casa 34, Av Rivadavia 550, 4th floor, T011-4342 5686, www.casa34.com. Helpful, with a big range.

Tu Casa Argentina, Esmeralda 980 2B, T011-4312 4127, www.tucasargentina.com. Furnished flats by the day, week or month; from about US$400 per month.

❷ Eating

Eating out in Buenos Aires is one of the city's great pleasures, with a huge variety of restaurants from the chic to the cheap, and lots of eclectic and exotic choices alongside the inevitable *parrilla* restaurant where you can eat the legendary huge Argentine steak, grilled to perfection over a wood fire. Argentines are very sociable and love to eat out, so if a restaurant is full, it's usually a good sign. Remember, though, that they'll usually start eating between 2130 and 2230. If in doubt, head for Puerto Madero, where there are lots of good mid-range places serving international as well as local cuisine. There are good deals at lunchtime in many restaurants where the *menú del día* costs US$4-7 for 2 courses and coffee. The following list gives only those restaurants easily accessible for people staying in the city centre. Wherever you're staying, take a Radio Taxi to Palermo or Las Cañitas for a wide range of excellent restaurants all within strolling distance. For more information on the gastronomy of Buenos Aires

see these helpful websites: www.guiaoleo.com.ar, restaurant guide in Spanish and English; www.vidalbuzzi.com.ar, great guide in Spanish. 2 fantastic food-orientated blogs written in English are: www.saltshaker.net, by chef Dan Perlman who also runs a highly recommended private restaurant in his house, see website for details; and www.buenosairesfoodies.com.

City centre *p29, map p32*

$$$ La Chacra, Av Córdoba 941 (just off 9 de Julio). A superb traditional *parrilla* with excellent steaks brought sizzling to your table, impeccable old-fashioned service and a lively buzzing atmosphere.

$$$ Morizono, Reconquista 899. Japanese sushi and sashami, as well as other dishes.

$$$ Sorrento Corrientes 668 (just off Florida). Intimate, elegant atmosphere, with dark wood, nicely lit tables, serving traditional menu with good fish dishes and steak.

$$ Broccolino, Esmeralda 776. Good Italian food, very popular, try *pechuguitas*.

$$ Club Español, Bernardo de Irigoyen 180 (on Av 9 de Julio, near Av de Mayo). Faded splendour in this fine old Spanish social club serving excellent seafood.

$$ Dadá, San Martín 941. Both a restaurant and bar, and great for gourmet lunches such as prawn salad. Great eclectic decoration.

$$ El Palacio de la Papa Frita, Lavalle 735 and 954, Av Corrientes 1620. Great traditional place for a filling feed, with a large menu and quite atmospheric, despite the bright lighting.

$$ El Querandí, Perú 302 and Moreno. Good food in an intimate atmosphere in this historical place that was opened in the 1920s. Also a popular café, well known for its Gin Fizz, and as a tango venue.

$$ Empire Bar, Tres Sargentos 427. Serves slightly expensive but good Thai food in a tasteful atmosphere.

$$ Rocket, Rivadavia 1285, Mon-Fri. British-style restaurant serving food such as curry and fish pie.

$$ Tancat, Paraguay 645. Really authentic Basque food and delicious dishes from other Spanish regions. Recommended.

$ California Burrito Company, Lavalle 441, www.californiaburritoco.com, Mon-Fri. Huge Tex-Mex burritos, Corona beers, Margaritas, cheap tacos Tue nights. Highly recommended.

$ Gianni´s, Viamonte 834 and 25 de Mayo 757, daily 0900-1700. The set menu is an ideal lunch option, served in a renovated old house. Risottos and salads are very good.

$ Güerrín, Av Corrientes 1368. A Buenos Aires institution, serving incredibly cheap and filling slabs of pizza and *fainá* (chickpea polenta) which you eat standing up at a zinc bar. If you eat at a table you miss out on the colourful local life. Wonderful.

$ La Casona del Nonno, Lavalle 827. Popular with tourists for its cheap set-price menu, Italian-style food, cheap pastas and *parrilla*.

$ Las Cuartetas, Av Corrientes 838. Local pizza institution open early to very very late, with fantastic cheap pizzas and 1970s-style furniture. Highly recommended.

$ Pura Vida, Reconquista 516, www.pura vidabuenosaires.com, Mon-Fri. Use all natural ingredients in their salads, juices, sandwiches, wraps and soups. Recommended. There's also a branch in Recoleta.

Tea rooms, café-bars and ice-cream parlours

Café Tortoni, Av de Mayo 825-9, www.cafe tortoni.com.ar. This famous Buenos Aires café has been the elegant haunt of artists and writers for over 150 years: Carlos Gardel sang here and Borges was a regular. It's self-conscious of its tourist status these days, but still atmospheric, with marble columns, stained-glass ceilings, old leather chairs and photographs of its famous clientele on the walls. Excellent coffee and cakes, and good tea, all rather pricey, but worth a visit for the interesting *peña* evenings of poetry and music, and jazz and tango.

Clásica y Moderna, Av Callao 892. One of the city's most welcoming cafés, with a bookshop at the back. Lots of brick and wood, this has a great atmosphere and is good from breakfast right through to drinks at night, with live music Thu to Sat. Highly recommended.

Como en Casa, Riobamba 1239. Set in a lovely building with a black and white tiled courtyard with a small fountain. Gourmet salads, sandwiches and amazing cakes. Try the brie and sun-dried tomato pizzetta.

Confitería Ideal, Suipacha 384. One of the most atmospheric cafés in the city. Wonderfully old-fashioned 1930s interior, almost untouched, serving coffee and excellent cakes, good service. Upstairs, tango is taught in the afternoons and there's tango dancing at a *milonga* here afterwards, from 2200. Highly recommended.

El Gato Negro, Av Corrientes 1669. A lovely old traditional café serving a wide choice of coffees and teas, and good cakes. You can also buy a big range of spices here.

Puerto Madero *p36*

The revamped docks area is an attractive place to eat and to stroll along the water-front before dinner. There are good places here, generally in stylish interiors and with good service. Can be a little overpriced.

$$$ Asia de Cuba, Perina Dealessi 750, www.asiadecuba.com.ar. Stunning restaurant serving Asian-influenced dishes. Very attentive staff.

$$$ El Bistro + Cava, Martha Salotti 445, inside the Faena + Universe Hotel. Expensive but exquisite food with an experienced wine sommelier to assist in your choices. Highly recommended.

$$$ El Clan, Olga Cossettini 1501, www.el-clan.com.ar. Chandeliers, long curtains and shiny cutlery. Try the grilled salmon or the home-made pasta.

$$$ La Parolaccia, Nos 1052 and 1170. Excellent pasta and Italian-style dishes (seafood is the speciality at No 1170), executive lunch US$8 Mon-Fri, popular.

$$$-$$ i Fresh Market, Azucena Villaflor and Olga Cossettini. Fresh fruits and vegetables served in the most varied ways in this small, trendy restaurant and deli, from breakfast to dinner.

$$ La Parolaccia, 2 sister restaurants: a general bistro at Alicia Moreau de Justo No 1052, and the best seafood restaurant in Puerto Madero, at No 1160, serving fresh and deliciously cooked seafood in a lively brasserie atmosphere. Both places are very stylish, and very popular with *Porteños*. Bargain lunches during the week and superb pastas. Recommended.

Recoleta and Barrio Norte *p37, map p38*

$$$ Lola, Roberto M Ortiz 1805. Well known for superb pasta dishes, lamb and fish. Recommended.

$$$ Sirop, Pasaje del Correo, V López 1661, T011-4813 5900. Delightful chic design, delicious French-inspired food, superb patisseries too. Highly recommended.

$$$ Tandoor, La Prida 1293. Indian restaurant with seriously spicy food. Great service but slightly expensive. Recommended.

$$ El Sanjuanino, Posadas 1515. Atmospheric place offering the best of Argentina's dishes from the northwest: *humitas*, *tamale* and *empanadas*, as well as unusual game dishes.

$$ Rodi Bar, Vicente López 1900. Excellent *bife* and other dishes in this typical *bodegón*. A welcoming and unpretentious place.

$ La Madeleine, Av Santa Fe 1726, open 24 hrs. Great for cheap pasta in a bright and cheerful atmosphere. Recommended.

Tea rooms and ice-cream parlours

Alvear Palace, Av Alvear 1891, T011-4808 2949. Afternoon tea served in the garden restaurant, **L'Orangerie**. 3-tier cake stands filled with cucumber sandwiches and wonderful cakes. Highly recommended. Book ahead.

Café Victoria, Roberto M Ortiz 1865. Wonderful, old-fashioned café, popular with perfectly coiffed ladies sipping tea in a refined atmosphere. Great cakes.

Palermo *p40, map p41*

There are lots of chic restaurants and bars in Palermo Viejo, Palermo Hollywood and the Las Cañitas district (see below). It's a sprawling area, and lovely to walk around in the evenings. Take a taxi to one of these restaurants and walk around once you're in the area before deciding where to eat.

Palermo has lots of good cafés opposite the park, and there is fabulous ice cream at **Un' Altra Volta**, Av del Libertador 3060, T011-4805 1818.

$$$ Cabernet, Jorge Luis Borges 1757, T011-4831 3071. The smoked salmon and caviar blinis starter here is unmissable. Dine outside in the elegant terrace, fragrant with jasmine, and heated in winter, or in the more traditional clubby interior in this traditional *chorizo* house, given a cosmopolitan twist with purple walls. Sophisticated, traditional cuisine, a great wine list and good service. Worth the price for a special dinner.

$$$ Cluny, El Salvador 4618, T011-4831 7176. A great place for lunch, the menu is as stylish as the black and cream surroundings. Excellent home-made bread. The fish and pasta sauces are made up of exquisite combinations of flavours. One of Palermo's classiest restaurants, whether you dine in the bistro at the back, or chic white armchairs in the middle. Friendly staff, mellow music. Recommended.

$$$ Dominga, Honduras 5618, T011-4771 4443, www.domingarestaurant.com. Open evenings only. Elegant, excellent food from a short but creative menu, professional service, good wine list, ideal for a romantic meal or treat.

$$$ El Manto, Costa Rica 5801, T011-4774 2409, Mon-Sat lunch and dinner. The usual chic concrete look, but the food is exceptional: delicious Armenian dishes cooked by a real Armenian chef, in this spacious relaxed restaurant. Friendly service. Good for a quiet evening.

$$$ Janio, Malabia 1805, T011-4833 6540. With a great position overlooking Plaza Palermo Viejo and a lovely upstairs terrace, this was one of the fist Palermo restaurants. Open from breakfast until the early hours, this is a lively, laid-back place for lunch, with a good fixed-price menu, and more sophisticated Argentine cuisine in the evenings. A great place to meet for a drink.

$$ Bar 6, Armenia 1676 T011-4833 6807, Mon-Sat. One of the best chic, modern bars. Serves food in laid-back spacious surroundings, with bare concrete, bold colours and sofas upstairs for relaxing on. Excellent lunches, friendly atmosphere, good for a drink in the evening. Recommended.

$$ B-Blue, Armenia 1692, www.b-blue.com.ar. A trendy café with loads of healthy vegetarian food. Recommended. Wi-Fi.

$$ Bio, Humboldt 2199, T011-4774 3880. Open daily, but closed Mon for dinner. Situated on a sunny corner where you can sit outside, Bio servces delicious gourmet organic food. Fresh lime green decor and a friendly atmosphere.

$$ El Diamante, Malabia 1688, 1st floor, T011-4831 5735, Mon-Sat. Great loud music in this cosy restaurant and bar with a terrace upstairs for a party atmosphere, gay-friendly.

$$ El Preferido de Palermo, Borges and Guatemala, T011-4778 7101. Very popular *bodegón* serving both Argentine and Spanish-style dishes.

$$ Eterna Cadencia, Honduras 5574, T011-4774 4100, Tue-Sun 0900-2400. A real find, a great little café in a fabulous small bookshop with a wonderful selection of English classics and contemporary literature. Beautifully designed high ceilinged rooms

with comfortable sofas at the back. Great for a light lunch.

$$ Garum, Malabia 1721, T011-4831 6203. Elegant restaurant and wine bar in an imaginatively redesigned old house. Wine tastings and good Mediterranean food. Spacious rooms decorated with contemporary art exhibitions.

$$ Krishna, Malabia 1833. A small, intimate place serving very good Indian-flavoured vegetarian dishes.

$$ La Cabrera, Cabrera 5127/5099, www.parrillalacabrera.com.ar. You can't make reservations for this amazing *parrilla*, but they will offer you sparkling wine while you wait. The wait however shouldn't be too long as they now have 2 restaurants virtually next to each other. Fantastic for food and pasta. Huge portions.

$$ Mark's Deli, El Salvador 4701. Fabulous café/restaurant serving goodies such as huge salads, overflowing sandwiches and juices. Recommended.

$$ Miranda, Costa Rica and Fitz Roy, T011-4771 4255. Traditional *parrilla* in hip surroundings, with simple rustic design and a lively atmosphere in the evenings. Also offers pasta and a good wine list. Lunch is good value.

$$ Olsen, Gorriti 5870. Recommended Swedish-style restaurant with delicate food, great cocktails and a relaxing terrace outside.

$$ Omm, Honduras 5656, T011-4774 4224. Hip, cosy wine and tapas bar with great wines and good food. Open daily from 1800, happy hour from 1800-2100. Sister restaurant **Omm Carnes**, Costa Rica 5198, T011-4773 0954, for steak and meat dishes in a similarly trendy environment, open daily from 1100 but closed for dinner on Sun.

$$ Social Paraíso, Honduras 5182. A real find for a great lunch. Simple, delicious dishes served in a relaxed, chic atmosphere in this friendly place run by art collectors. Groovy paintings on the walls and a lovely little patio hidden at the back. Good fish and tasty salads. Recommended.

Persicco, Salguero and Cabello, Maure and Migueletes and Av Rivadavia 4933. Branches in upmarket areas, but most convenient is **Salguero** (near Alto Palermo shopping centre), Salguero 2591 y Cabello. 'The best ice cream in the world.' You haven't tasted ice cream until you've had Persicco's mascarpone, or their *flan de dulce de leche*. Exquisite chocolate flavours, fruity ice creams, sorbets and even coffee. Also offer a delivery service, T0810-333 7377, and free Wi-Fi.

Las Cañitas

Northeast of Palermo Hollywood, separated from it by a railway track, this has developed into a popular little area for eating, with a huge number of restaurants packed into a few blocks along Báez. Most open at around 2000, and also for lunch at weekends:
$$ Báez, next door to **Morella**. Very trendy, with lots of orange neon, serving sophisticated Italian-style food, including the delicious goat's cheese ravioli.
$$ Campo Bravo, Báez and Arevalo. A stylish, minimalist place serving superb steaks and vegetables on the *parrilla* in a friendly atmosphere. Popular and recommended.
$$ De la Ostia, Báez 212. A small and chic bistro for tapas and Spanish-style food, with a good atmosphere.
$$$ Eh! Santino, Báez 194. A trendy small restaurant for Italian-style food and drinks. Dark and cosy with lots of mirrors.
$$$ Morelia, Báez 260. Cooks superb pizzas on the *parrilla* or in wood ovens, and has a lovely roof terrace for summer.
$$$ Novecento. Across the road from **De la Ostia** is a lively French-style bistro, stylish but unpretentious. Serves good fish dishes among other things on the broad menu.

San Telmo *p43, map p44*

There are plenty of restaurants along Defensa and in the surrounding streets, and new places are opening all the time.

$$$ Defensa Al Sur, Defensa 1338, T011-4300 8017. Converted old shopfront, housing one of the poshest restaurants in the area. Wonderful wines and a modern twist on local dishes. Recommended.
$$$ La Brigada, Estados Unidos 465, T011-4361 5557. The best choice for *parrilla* in San Telmo, this is a really superb and atmospheric *parrilla*, serving excellent Argentine cuisine and wines in a cosy, buzzing atmosphere. Very popular and not cheap, but highly recommended. Always reserve in advance.
$$ Brasserie Pétanque, Defensa y México, T011-4342 7930. Very good French cuisine at affordable prices and set lunch Mon-Fri. It's an appealing little place, a tasteful combination of Paris and Buenos Aires.
$$ Café San Juan, Av San Juan 450, T011-4300 1112. Not a café but a very small *bodegón* – lookng just like a typical *restaurant de barrio* (local dive) but with an excellent cook. A short menu includes delicious *tapas de salmón*. It's very popular so book ahead.
$$ La Vinería de Gualterio Bolívar, Bolívar 865, T011-4361 4709. Serving tiny portions of tapas-like dishes which are delicious, this small restaurant also boasts efficient staff and an extensive wine list. Recommended.
$$ Los Lobos, corner of Estados Unidos and Balcarce. Attractive restaurant, simply designed, serving modern fare such as spinach and camembert omelette. Good for lunch.
$ Bar Británico, Brasil and Defensa 399, T11-43612107. Open 24 hrs, with a long and impressive history behind it. Worth the walk to soak up the atmosphere over lunch.
$ El Desnivel, Defensa 855. Popular for cheap and basic food, packed at weekends.
$ La Trastienda, Balcarce 460. Theatre café with lots of live events. Also serves meals and drinks from breakfast till dinner, great music. A relaxed place to hang out with an arty crowd. Recommended.
$ Pride Cafe, corner of Balcarce and Giuffra. Wonderful sandwiches, juices, salads and great brownies. Lots of magazines to read.

$ El Hipopótamo, Brasil and Defensa (on Parque Lezama). A typical *bodegón*, popular with families. Argentine menu and huge portions. The service is rather slow.
$ Nonna Bianca, Estados Unidos 425. Great ice cream, as well as an internet café.

🎵 Bars and clubs

Generally it is not worth going to clubs before 0230 at weekends. Dress is usually smart, and you can be charged anything from US$10-15 sometimes including a drink. Most gay clubs charge US$10 entry on the door.

City centre *p29, map p32*
Bars
See also under Live music, below.
Druid In, Reconquista 1040. Live music weekly, English spoken.
La Cigale, 25 de Mayo 722. A popular place after office hrs that's usually crowded by 2400. Very good music, recommended for its Tue evenings with guest DJs.
Le Bar, Tucumán 422. Busy, 2-level cocktail bar which attracts the after office crowd and is a great unpretentious place to chill out.

Recoleta *p37, map p38*
Bars
Buller Brewing Company, Roberto M Ortiz 1827. Happy hour till 2100.
Casa Bar, Rodríguez Peña 1150. Offering beers from all over the world, this restored French mansion is a good place to watch international sports matches. Affordable food deals.
Milion, Paraná 1048. A French-style residence with lots of space, sitting areas, cushions and tables in the sumptuous halls. It has also a garden and serves very good drinks. A mixed clientele, between 25 and 40 years old. Recommended Fri after midnight.
The Shamrock, Rodríguez Peña 1220. Irish-run, popular, expensive Guinness, happy hour for ISIC card holders.

Clubs
El Living, Marcelo T de Alvear 1540, T011-4811 4730. As small, cosy and relaxed as a living room gets, playing 1980s music amongst others.

Palermo *p40, map p41*
Bars
878, Thames 878. From the outside this doesn't look like a bar, but knock on the door after 2400 and you'll be invited inside to a cosy red room filled with people. Recommended.
Bangalore Pub, Humboldt 1416, and Niceto Vega. Great English pub serving wonderful mojitos and wraps. Also serve curries.
Carnal, Niceto Vega 5511 and Humboldt. Busy roof terrace that is great in summer, with good music and a bar downstairs.
Congo, Honduras 5329. Huge bar which extends to a large beer garden at the back. Interesting crowd and a good range of cocktails. Men usually have to pay a US$6 cover charge redeemable for drinks.
Mundo Bizarro, Serrano 1222 and Córdoba. This hugely popular bar gets its name from bizarre films shown on a big screen. People usually come here for dinner first (food is American-style), then they stay all night. DJ on Fri and Sat; 1960s and 1980s music the rest of the week. 20- to 35-year-old crowd.
Sugar, Costa Rica 4619. Welcoming bar with lots of red and wood to make it feel cosy. Cheapest beer and drinks in Palermo. Happy hour every night. Friendly crowd.

Clubs
Club 69 (at Niceto Club), Niceto Vega 5510, T011-4779 9396, www.nicetoclub.com, or www.club69.com.ar. On Thu for a 20-something crowd, good music with live shows, packed after 0200.
Mint, Av Costanera Norte and Sarmiento (in Punta Carrasco). On Sat, Latin and electronic music. Mostly 20-somethings. Attractive terrace on the river.

Pacha, Av Costanera Norte and Pampa, www.pachabuenosaires.com. A big place, upmarket feel, 20- to 30-year-olds, electronic music.

Gay bars and clubs
Bach Bar, Cabrera 4390, www.bach-bar.com.ar. Friendly lesbian bar in Palermo Viejo.
Sitges, Av Córdoba 4119, T011-4861 2763, www.sitgesonline.com.ar. Gay and lesbian bar, near **Amerika**.

San Telmo *p43, map p44*
Bars
A great way to visit some of the best bars is to join a pub crawl. A good company to contact is Pub Crawl BA (www.pubcrawlba.com) who run pub crawls every week. It's a good way to make friends and have a safe night out.
70 Living, Defensa 714. Good terrace with well-made cocktails, and a great atmosphere with DJs spinning smooth beats.
Bar Dorrego, Humberto Primo and Defensa. This bar/café has a fantastic atmosphere and waiters inside, and you can also sit in the plaza outside. Good for late-night coffees or beers.
Bar Seddon, corner of Defensa and Chile. Wonderful traditional bar open till late with live music on Fri nights. Candles, high ceilings, as well as black and white tiles on the floor. Recommended.
Gibraltar, Perú 895. Small British pub with a tiny beer garden, a pool table and happy hour at 1800-2000 each night. Popular with tourists and locals alike, it is best to go either really early at 1800 or late about 0130. Try the green curry or the pie.
La Puerta Roja, Chacabuco 733. No sign outside but ring the doorbell and climb the marble stairs. Stylishly designed bar serving pints, great food (wraps and curries) and open till late. Recommended.
La Resistencia, Defensa and Independencia. Local hangout that serves cheap beer and plays lots of rock music. A fun night out and a chance to speak some Spanish.

Plan B, Brasil 444, a short walk from Plaza Dorrego. This alternative bar doesn't look much from the outside but it is actually a converted house, with high ceilings, peeling paint and friendly hosts. You can bring your own music, and there is a pool table.

Clubs
Museum, Perú between Chile and México. Absolutely huge club, which packs out on Wed 'After Office' nights, from 2100 until about 0200.

Gay bars and clubs
Amerika, Gascón 1040, Almagro, T011-4865 4416, www.ameri-k.com.ar. The largest gay club which draws over 2000 party-goers spread over 3 floors.

🌀 Entertainment

Details of most events are given in the 'Espectáculos' section of newspapers, *La Nación* and *Clarín*, the *Buenos Aires Herald* (English) on Fri, and the helpful www.whatsupbuenosaires.com.

Cinemas
The selection of films shown in Buenos Aires is excellent, ranging from new Hollywood releases to Argentine and world cinema; details are listed daily in all main newspapers. Films are shown uncensored and in the original language, with most foreign films subtitled rather than dubbed into Spanish: only children's films are dubbed. Check this before buying tickets though. Tickets are best booked in the early afternoon to ensure good seats (average price US$5.50, more expensive at weekends and as much as US$6.50 on Sat night; there are discounts on Wed and for 1st show daily, but other discounts depend on the cinema). Most shopping malls have cinemas and these tend to show more mainstream Hollywood movies, but you can find recent European or non-Hollywood films elsewhere, mostly in the Atlas chain of

cinemas: **Arteplex**, Av Cabildo 2829, T011-4781 6500, Belgrano; **Cineduplex**, Av Rivadavia 5050, T011-4902 5682; and **Lorca**, Av Corrientes 1428. Old movies, classics, curiosities and experimental cinema are shown at **MALBA art gallery**, Av Figueroa Alcorta 3415, T011-4808 6500, and at **Sala Leopoldo Lugones** (Teatro San Martín), Av Corrientes 1530, 10th floor, T011-4371 0111. Most Argentinian movies are shown at **Complejo Tita Merello**, Suipacha 442, T011-4322 1195, and at **Gaumont**, Av Rivadavia 1635, T011-4371 3050.

For what's on in all cinemas throughout Buenos Aires, see any daily paper or websites such as www.lanacion.com.ar, www.buenosairesherald.com, or www.terra.com.ar. Independent foreign and national films are shown during the **Festival de Cine Independiente**, held every Apr.

Cultural events and activities
Centro Cultural Borges, Galerías Pacífico, Viamonte and San Martín, www.ccborges.org.ar. Music and dance concerts, special exhibitions, some offer student discounts.
Centro Cultural Recoleta, Junín 1930, next to the Recoleta cemetery, www.centro culturalrecoleta.org. Many free activities.
Ciudad Cultural Konex, Sarmiento 3131, Abasto, www.ciudadculturalkonex.org. A fantastic converted industrial site, the most popular event is the Fiesta la Bomba de Tiempo, US$4 – a passionate drum and beat show that starts at midnight. Highly recommended.
Fundación Proa, Av Pedro de Mendoza 1979, www.proa.org. Contemporary art in La Boca.
Luna Park stadium, Bouchard 465, www.lunapark.com.ar. Pop/jazz concerts, sports events, ballet and musicals.
Palais de Glace, Posadas 1725, www.palaisdeglace.org. Temporary art exhibitions, especially photography and other cultural events.

Teatro Colón, www.teatrocolon.org.ar. Newly renovated and bursting with great events. See the website for details.
Teatro San Martín, Corrientes 1530, www.teatrosanmartin.com.ar. Organizes cultural activities, many free, including concerts. 50% ISIC discount for Thu, Fri and Sun events (only in advance at 4th floor, Mon-Fri). The theatre's **Sala Leopoldo Lugones** shows international classic films, daily, US$2.

Live music
La Peña del Colorado, Güemes 3657, T011-4822 1038. Argentinean *folclore* music played live in this atmospheric and cheerful place, where regional food is served. Recommended.
La Trastienda, Balcarce 460. This popular venue attracts a mixed crowd for very different types of music.
Maluco Beleza, Sarmiento 1728. Live Brazilian dance music.
Mítico Argentino Humberto, Primo 489. In the heart of San Telmo. Although it is tourist-central around Plaza Dorrego, you'll rub shoulders with lots of Argentines as well.
ND Ateneo, Paraguay 918. A small theatre for a great variety of Latin American music.
Niceto, Niceto Vega 5510 (Palermo Hollywood district) and **La Cigale**, 25 de Mayo 722, T011-4312 8275.

Jazz
Café Tortoni, Av de Mayo 825, T011-4342 4328, www.cafetortoni.com.ar. Features the Fénix Jazz Band (Dixieland), Sat 2300.
La Revuelta, Alvarez Thomas 1368, T011-4553 5530. Live jazz, bossa nova and tango.
Notorious, Av Callao 966, T011-4813 6888, www.notorious.com.ar. Music shop and live music.
Thelonious, Salguero 1884, T011-4829 1562. Atmospheric jazz bar serving snacks and good cocktails.

Tango

There are basically 2 ways to enjoy Buenos Aires' wonderfully sensuous and passionate dance: watch superb tango at a show, or learn to dance at a class and then try your new steps at a *milonga* (tango club). Tango may seem impossibly complicated, but it's the key to the Argentine psyche, and you haven't experienced the dance unless you've tried it on the dance floor.

There is a tango information desk at the **Centro Cultural San Martín**, Sarmiento 1551, T011-4373 2829, daily 1400-2100, and a useful website: www.tangoguia.com. Look out for the latest leaflet listing tango classes and *milongas*, *Passionate Buenos Aires*, produced by the city tourist board, and available from tourist information kiosks.

Tango shows

This is the way to see tango dancing at its best. Most shows pride themselves on a very high level of dancing, and although they're not cheap, this could be the highlight of your visit.
Bar Sur, Estados Unidos 299, T011-4362 6086. 2000-0300, US$60 including all-you-can-eat pizza, drinks extra. Good fun, and the public sometimes join the professional dancers.
Café Tortoni, see cafés above. Daily tango shows from 2030, US$12.
El Cabaret at Faena Hotel and Universe, Martha Salotti 445, T011-4010 9200. A glamorous and sensual show, charting tango's evolution, daily at 2030.
El Querandí, Perú 302, T011-5199 1770. Elaborate tango show restaurant, daily, dinner 2030, show at 2215, US$100 for both, including a transfer from your hotel.
El Viejo Almacén, Independencia and Balcarce, T011-4307 7388. The best place of all. Daily, with dinner from 2030, show at 2200, US$105 with all included, or US$58 show only (recommended). Very impressive dancing from the city's best dancers, excellent live band and great singing from

some of tango's great names. Highly recommended.
La Esquina de Carlos Gardel, Carlos Gardel 3200, T011-4867 6363, www.esquinacarlos gardel.com.ar. Dinner at 2030 and show at 2215, US$108 for both, US$76 show only. Recommended.
La Ventana, Balcarce 431, T011-4331 0217. Daily dinner from 2000 (dinner and show US$100) or show with 2 drinks, 2200, US$55. Touristy but very good, and the only show to include some of Argentina's traditional *folclore* music.
Piazzolla Tango, Florida 165 (basement), Galería Güemes, T011-4344 8200, www. piazzollatango.com. A beautifully restored belle époque hall hosts a smart tango show; dinner at 2045 (dinner and show US$98), show at 2215 (show only US$53).
Tangol, Florida 971, p 1, T011-4312 7276, www.tangol.com, see also Tour operators, page 68. Run trips to tango shows.

Milongas and tango classes

Milongas are extremely popular among younger *Porteños*, since tango underwent a revival a few years ago. You can take a class and get a good feel for the music, before the dancing starts a couple of hours later. Both traditional tango and *milonga* (a more cheerful style of music with a faster rhythm) are played, and venues occasionally have live orchestras. Cost is usually around US$4, and even complete beginners are welcome. Tango classes are also given all over the city, but you might find *milongas* more fun, and they're better places to meet people.
Central Cultural Torquato Tasso, Defensa 1575, T011-4307 6506. Daily evening classes, dancing Sun at 2100. English spoken.
Confitería Ideal, Suipacha 384, T011-5265 8069. Dancing Mon, Wed, Sat and Sun. Daily classes from 1500.
Dandi, Piedras 936, T011-4361 3537, www.mansiondandiroyal.com. Excellent teaching with Noelia and Nahuel or Rodolfo

and Irma. Mon, Tue, Fri 1900, Wed 1800, Sat 1700, Sun 1930, 2200.

La Catedral, Sarmiento 4006. A wonderful old church hall, with eclectic furniture and a wonderful restaurant. Lessons start at 2100, and then it turns into a milonga after 2230. US$4 entrance fee includes both. Sometimes there are singing and tango performances as well. Don't be put off by the plain frontage.

La Viruta, Armenia 1366, Palermo Viejo, T011-4774 6357, www.lavirutatango.com. Most popular among a young trendy crowd. Wed, 2300, Fri and Sat 2400. Classes Wed 2130, Thu 2000 (includes tango and *milonga* lessons), Fri and Sat 2230, Sun 2000 (includes *milonga* and tango lessons).

Porteño y Bailarín, Riobamba 345, T011-4932 5452, www.porteybailarin.com.ar. Tue and Sun class 2100, dancing 2300.

Theatre

About 20 commercial theatres play all year, and there are many amateur theatres, with a theatre festival at the end of May. The main theatre street is Av Corrientes which has miles and miles of side-by-side theatres. Check out *La Nación* for theatre times. You are advised to book early for a seat at a concert, ballet or opera. Tickets for most popular shows (including rock and pop concerts) are sold also through **Entrada Plus**, T011-4324 1010; **Ticketek**, T011-5237 7200, www.ticketek. com.ar. See www.alternativa teatral.com, or www.mundoteatral.com.ar. For listings, see www.terra.com.ar, www.lanacion.com, www.buenosairesherald.com.

The following includes the main theatres, almost all of them in the centre. **Beckett Teatro**, Guardia Vieja 3556, T011-4867 5185; **Broadway**, Av Corrientes 1155, T011-4381 1180; **Centro Cultural Borges**, Viamonte and San Martín, T011-5555 5359; **Centro Cultural de la Cooperación**, Av Corrientes 1543, T011-5077 8077; **Ciudad Cultural Konex**, Sarmiento 3131, T011-5237 7200, www.ciudadculturalkonex.org; **Coliseo**,

Marcelo T de Alvear 1125, T011-4816 3789; **El Nacional**, Av Corrientes 960, T011-4326 4218; **General San Martín**, Av Corrientes 1530, T0800-333 5254; **La Plaza**, Av Corrientes 1660, T011-6320 5350; **Liceo**, Rivadavia and Paraná, T011-4381 5745; **Lola Membrives**, Av Corrientes 1280, T011-4381 0076; **Maipo**, Esmeralda 443, T011-4322 4882; **Multiteatro**, Av Corrientes 1283, T011-4382 9140; **Nacional Cervantes**, Libertad 815, T011- 4816 4224; **Opera**, Av Corrientes 860, T011-4326 1335; **Payró**, San Martín 766, T011-4312 5922; **Regina**, Av Santa Fe 1235, T011-4812 5470; Teatro Colón, www.teatrocolon.org.ar. **Teatro del Globo**, Marcelo T de Alvear 1155, T011-4816 3307; **Teatro del Pueblo**, Av Roque Sáenz Peña 943, T011-4326 3606.

O Shopping

Contemporary Argentine design is excellent, with fashionable cuts and fabrics which would hold their own in London or Milan but at a third of the price. Argentine designers make the most of the superb quality leather for jackets, shoes and bags, ranging from the funky to the classic and traditional.

Palermo is the best place for chic little boutiques and some well-known international names, with shops spread out through pleasant leafy streets with lots of cafés (see below for details). For the major names, head straight to **Patio Bullrich**, an upmarket indoor shopping mall. In the centre of town, the main shopping streets are the pedestrianized **Florida**, stretching south from Plaza San Martín, and the whole of **Santa Fe**, from Av 9 de Julio to Av Pueyrredon, though some blocks are more upmarket than others, and there are some obviously cheaper zones. Palermo is so full of boutiques and chic interiors shops you will be spoilt for choice, and it's hard to know where to start. The 2 main shopping streets to head for, then, are **Honduras** and

El Salvador, between Malabia and Serrano, with more options further south on Gorriti and along Costa Rica.

To get the tax back on purchases, see Essentials, page 19.

Antiques

There are many high quality antiques for sale around Recoleta: a stroll along the streets around Callao and Quintana will yield some great buys. For cheaper antiques, and second-hand bric-a-brac, San Telmo is the place. The market on Sun is a good place to start, but on other days all the shops along Defensa are still open, and it's worth searching around for bargains. China, glass, rugs, old silver *mates*, clothes and jewellery are among the goodies you can pick up.

Pasaje de la Defensa, Defensa 1179. A beautifully restored 1880s house containing small shops.

Books

You'll find most bookshops along Florida, Av Corrientes or Av Santa Fe, and in shopping malls. Second-hand and discount bookshops are mostly along Av Corrientes and Av de Mayo. Rare books are sold in several specialized stores in the Microcentro (the area enclosed by Suipacha, Esmeralda, Tucumán and Paraguay). The main chains of bookshops to look for, usually selling a small selection of foreign books, are: **Cúspide**, with several branches on Florida, Av Corrientes and some malls, and the biggest and most interesting store at Village Recoleta, Vicente López and Junín; **Distal**, Florida 738 and more branches on Florida and Av Corrientes; **Yenny-El Ateneo**, in all shopping malls, also sell music. The biggest store is on Av Santa Fe 1860 set in an amazing old theatre, it is one of the best bookshops in South American, there is café where the stage should be, and it extends 3 floors up.

For a larger selection of books in English, try the following:

Eterna Cadencia, Honduras 5574, T011-4774 4100. Great bookshop with excellent selection of novels in English: classics, contemporary fiction and translations of Spanish and Argentine authors. Highly recommended for its café too.

Crack Up, Costa Rica 4767, T011-4831 3502. Funky, open-plan bookshop and café that extends to the street. Open Mon-Wed till 2230, and till the early hrs the rest of the week.

Walrus Books, Estados Unidos 617, T011-4300 713. Shop in San Telmo with second-hand books in English, including Latin American authors. Good children's section.

You can also try **ABC**, Maipú 866; **Joyce, Proust & Co**, Tucumán 1545 p 1 A, also sells books in other European languages; **Kel**, Marcelo T de Alvear 1369; **Librería Rodríguez**, Sarmiento 835; **LOLA**, Viamonte 976, Mon-Fri 1200-1830, small publishers specializing in Latin America natural history, also sell used and rare editions, most in English.

Foreign newspapers are available from news-stands on Florida, in Recoleta and the kiosk at Corrientes and Maipú.

Camping equipment

Angel Baraldo, Av Belgrano 270, www.baraldo. com.ar. Imported and Argentine stock.

Buenos Aires Sports, Panamericana and Paraná, Martínez (Shopping Unicenter, 2nd level). Good equipment.

Cacique Camping, Esteban Echeverría 3360, Munro, T011-47624475, caciquenet@ ciudad.com.ar. Clothing and equipment.

Camping Center, Esmeralda 945, www. camping-center.com.ar. Good selection of outdoor sports gear and equipment.

Ecrin, Mendoza 1679, T011-4784 4799, www.ecrin.com.ar. Sells imported climbing equipment.

Fugate (no sign), Gascón 238 (off Rivadavia 4000 block), T011-4982 0203. Also repairs equipment.

Jorge Gallo, Liniers 1522, Tigre, T011- 4731 0323. For GPS repair service.

Montagne, Florida 719, Paraná 834, www.montagenoutdoors.com.ar. Good selection of outdoor sports gear and equipment.

Outside Mountain Equipment, Otero 172 (Chacarita), T011-4856 6204, www.outside.com.ar.

Camping gas available at: **Britam**, B Mitre 1111; **El Pescador**, Paraguay and Libertad; **Todo Gas**, Sarmiento 1540.

Clothes and accessories
The following can all be found in Palermo.

Men's clothes and accessories
Airborn, Gurruchaga 1770. Informal and more formal clothes.

Balthazar, Gorriti 5131. Smart men's clothes and accessories.

Etiqueta Negra, www.etiquetanegra.us. An Argentine clothing label that produces classic styles with a twist. Find them at all shopping malls.

Il Reve, Gurruchaga 1867. Smart, well-tailored and original menswear.

Postman, Armenia 1555. Great leather postman's bags and wallets.

Sartori, Gurruchaga 1538. Shoes with a baseball/camper feel.

Women's clothes and accessories
Caro Cuore, Armenia 1535. Great underwear, alluring and beautifully designed, and much cheaper than in Europe. Vast, calm shop where the staff are really helpful.

Colombas, Jorge Luis Borges 2029. Fabulous handmade jewellery, eclectic, hippy and very original styles, as well as lovely chic hand-knitted jumpers.

Elementos, El Salvador 4817. Soft minimalist suede and leather bags.

Josefina Ferroni, Armenia 1471. Chic shoes.

María Blizniuk, Costa Rica and Borges. Lovely feminine designs, cute shoes too.

Mariana Dappianno, Honduras 4932. Interesting and elegant designer, novel textiles.

Mariano Toledo, Armenia 1564, www.marianotoledo.com. Very elegant, unusual and feminine modern designs, innovative fabrics and cuts. See website for inspiration.

Nueveveinticinco (925), Honduras 4808, www.nueveveinticinco.com.ar. Fabulous jewellery shop where the owners create wonderful contemporary designs around stunning rocks of all kinds, and also to your specifications. Incredible value.

Rapsodia, El Salvador 4757. Great range of this best selling eclectic brand of eccentric clothes. Wonderful jeans and helpful staff who rush around and get your size.

Renzo Rainero, Gurruchaga and Honduras. High-quality leather and interesting designs.

Uma, Honduras 5225. Stylish and contemporary leather.

Handicrafts
Alhué, Juncal 1625. Very good indigenous-style crafts.

Art Petrus, Florida 969, and **Hotel Panamericano** at Carlos Pellegrini.

Arte y Esperanza, Balcarce 234. Excellent little shop selling an impressive range of indigenous crafts from all over Argentina, particularly the northwest. Chaguar bags, masks and weavings. Ethical owners give most of the profits back to the communities who make the goods. Standard is high and prices are reasonable. Highly recommended.

El Boyero, Galería Larreta, Florida 953. High quality silver, leather, wood work and other typical Argentine handicrafts.

Martín Fierro, Santa Fe 992. Good handicrafts, stonework, etc. Recommended.

Plata Nativa, Galería del Sol, Florida 860, local 41, www.platanativa.com. For Latin American folk handicrafts.

Interiors

There are fabulous interior design shops throughout Palermo, of which just a couple are mentioned, since it's assumed you won't be able to take much home with you. Look out for the free shopping guides which list the Palermo shops and show them on a map.

Arte Etnico Argentino, El Salvador 4600. Great collection of indigenous art from all over Argentina. High quality and reasonable prices, given that they're a little higher than you'd pay in the place of origin. Weavings, especially, are superb.

Calma Chicha, Honduras 4925, and a smaller branch at Defensa and Guiffra in San Telmo, www.calmachicha.com. The name means calm before the storm, and this is the 1 place you should browse in for gifts to bring home. Wonderful minimalist cowhide postman's bags and wallets, seats and table mats – or buy an entire cowhide! Also loads of chic kitsch, like the 'Hand of God' flick books that endlessly replay Maradona's immortal moment, plus tin *mates* and cute toys.

Leather

As you'd expect from all the cattle Argentina produces, leather is cheap and of very high quality here.

Aida, Galería de la Flor, shop 30, Florida 670. Here you can have a leather jacket made to measure in the same day.

Campanera Dalla Fontana, Reconquista 735. A leather factory producing fast, efficient and reasonably priced made-to-measure clothes.

Casa López, Marcelo T de Alvear 640/658. The most traditional and finest leather shop, expensive but worth it.

Galería del Caminante, Florida 844. A variety of good shops with leather goods, arts and crafts, souvenirs, etc.

Prüne, Florida 963, and in many shopping centres. Fashionable designs for bags, boots and shoes. Lots of choice, reasonably priced.

Uma, in shopping malls and at Honduras 5225 (Palermo Viejo). The trendiest of all.

Quality inexpensive leather goods are available at **All Horses**, Suipacha 1350; and at **La Curtiembre**, Juncal 1173, Paraguay 670.

Markets

Markets can be found all over Buenos Aires, since many plazas and parks have fairs at weekends where you can find almost the same kind of handicrafts everywhere. The following are recommended for something different:

Feria de las Artes, on Defensa, around Alsina, Fri 1200-1700. A few stalls selling crafts.

Feria de Mataderos, Av de los Corrales 6436, T011-4687 1949, www.feriademataderos. com.ar, Sun 1100-2000. Traditional gaucho crafts and games. See Around Buenos Aires, page 76, for more about Mataderos.

Mercado de las Luces, in the Manzana de las Luces, Perú and Alsina, Mon-Fri 1100-1900, Sun 1400-1900. Handicrafts.

Parque Centenario, Díaz Vélez and L Marechal. Sat market, with local crafts and good, cheap hand-made clothes.

Parque Rivadavia, Rivadavia 4900. Books and magazines, daily; records, toys, stamps and coins, Sun 0900-1300.

Plaza Dorrego, San Telmo. A wonderfully atmospheric market for souvenirs, antiques and some curious bric-a-brac. Free tango performances and live music, Sun 1300-2000.

Plaza Italia, Santa Fe and Uriarte (Palermo). Second-hand textbooks and magazines are sold daily; handicrafts market on Sat 1200-2000, Sun 1000-2000.

Recoleta, just outside the cemetery. At weekends, a huge craft market is held, with lots of street performers and food on sale too. Recommended.

Shopping malls

Alcorta, Salguero 3172. Massive mall with everything, plus supermarkets and some cheaper shops. Hard to reach without a car though.

Alto Palermo, Av Santa Fe and Coronel Díaz. Nearest *Subte* opposite Bulnes, Line D. Great for all the main clothes chain stores, and about 10 blocks' walk from Palermo's boutiques.

Galerias Pacificos, corner of Florida and Córdoba, nearest *Subte* Plaza San Martín on Line C, Mon-Sat 1000-2100, Sun 2100-2100. Has a good range of everything and a food court in the basement.

Patio Bullrich, Posadas 1245, nearest *Subte* 8 blocks from Plaza San Martín, Line C. The city's most upmarket mall, with all the international designer names and the best Argentine designers too. Also valet parking, taxi service and small food court in very elegant surroundings.

Unicenter, Paraná 3745, Martínez, www.unicenter.com.ar, no *Subte* anywhere near but you can take the No 60 bus from the city for about an hr or take a taxi, US$9. Has everything you could possibly imagine in one overwhelming place. Take a flask of brandy, this is the biggest shopping centre in South America.

▲▲ Activities and tours

Bicycle hire and tours
La Bicicleta Naranja, Pasaje Giuffra 308, San Telmo, www.labibibletanajanja.com.ar. Bike hire and bike tours to all parts of the city, 4-5 hrs.

Lan&Kramer Bike Tours, T011-4311 5199, www.biketours.com.ar. Starts daily at 0930 and 1400 next to the monument of San Martín (Plaza San Martín), 3½- to 4-hr cycle tours to the south or the north of the city; also to San Isidro and Tigre, 4½-5 hrs, and rent bikes at Florida 868,14H.

Urban biking, Moliere 2801 (Villa Devoto) T011-45684321, www.urbanbiking.com. 4-hr cycle tours starting next to the English clock tower in Retiro, light lunch included, also night city tours, and day tours to San Isidro and Tigre. They also rent bikes and organize cycle tours in the Pampas.

Boat trips
Barbacharters, T011-4824 3366. Boat trips and fishing in the delta and Tigre areas.

Smile on Sea, T011-155 018 8662 (mob), www.smileonsea.com. 2-hr boat trips off Buenos Aires coast in the day and at sunset, leaving from Puerto Madero on 32-ft sailing boats (up to 5 passengers). Also 8-hr trips to San Isidro and delta and longer holidays along the Uruguayan coast.

Cricket
Cricket is played Nov-Mar. More information at **Asociación de Cricket Argentino**, Paraguay 1270, T011-4816 3569.

Football and rugby
Football season is Mar-Jul, Aug-Dec, matches on Sun and sometimes on Wed, Fri or Sat.

Fans of the beautiful game should see **Boca Juniors**, matches every 2nd Sun 1500-1900 at their stadium, **La Bombonera**, Brandsen 805, La Boca, www.bocajuniors. com.ar. Cheapest tickets US$7. For details of the museum, see page 46. Try to see the murals along Av Almirante Brown. Take buses 29, 33, 53, 64, 86, 152, 168; along Av Patricios buses 10, 39, 93. Do not take a bus if travelling alone: call a Radio Taxi. Or you could walk. Their arch-rivals are the slightly upmarket **River Plate**, www.carp.org.ar, and they also have a museum near the stadium, daily 1000-1900, www.museoriver.com. To reach the stadium and the museum take bus No 29 from centre going north.

Rugby season Apr-Oct/Nov. See also **Tangol** under Tour operators, page 68.

Golf
Those wishing to play at the private golf clubs should bring handicap certificate and make telephone booking. There are about a dozen clubs. Weekend play possible with a member. Some hotels may be able to arrange.

Campo de Golf de la Ciudad in Palermo, open to anyone. For information contact, **Asociación Argentina de Golf**, T011-4325 1113.

Helicopter rides
Patagonia Chopper, www.patagonia chopper.com.ar. Helitours of Buenos Aires and its surroundings, 15-45 mins.

Horse racing and horse riding
At **Hipódromo Argentino de Palermo**, a large, modern racecourse, popular throughout the year; and at **San Isidro**. Riding schools at both courses.
Turismo Feeling, San Martín 969, p 9, T011-4313 5533, www.feelingturismo.com.ar. Excellent and reliable horseback trips in the Andes, and adventure tourism.

Motor racing
There are stock racing and Formula 3 competitions Mar-Dec, and drag racing year round, Fri evenings at the **Oscar Alfredo Gálvez Autodrome**, Av Coronel Roca and Av General Paz, T011-4605 3333, www.autodromoba.com.ar.

Polo
Argentina has the top polo players in the world. The high handicap season is Sep-Dec, but it is played all year round (low season is May-Aug). A visit to the national finals at Palermo in Nov and Dec is recommended. For information, **Asociación Argentina de Polo**, T011-4777 6444, www.aapolo.com.

Swimming
Public baths near **Aeroparque**, **Punta Carrasco**, and **Parque Norte**, both popular. **Club de Amigos**, Av Figueroa Alcorta and Av Sarmiento, T011-4801 1213, open all year round.

Tour operators
An excellent way of seeing Buenos Aires and its surroundings is on a 3-hr tour, especially for those travelling alone, or concerned about security. Longer tours might include dinner and a tango show, or a trip to an *estancia* (farm or ranch), with excellent food. Bookable through most travel agents.
Argentina Excepcion, Juncal 4455, Floor 5, 'A', T011-4772 6620, www.argentina- excepcion. com. A friendly French/Argentine- owned agency that offers individually tailored holidays around Argentina. They also offer themed holidays: fishing, golf, tango and trekking.
ATI, Esmeralda 567, T011-5217 9030, www.ativiajes.com. Mainly group travel, very efficient, many branches.
BAT, Buenos Aires Tur, Lavalle 1444, office 10, T011-4371 2304, www.buenosaires tur.com. City tours twice daily; Tigre and delta, daily, 6 hrs.
Buenos Aires Vision, Esmeralda 356 p 8, T011-4394 4682, www.buenosaires-vision. com.ar. City tours, Tigre and delta, tango (cheaper without dinner) and Fiesta Gaucha.
Cicerones de Buenos Aires, J J Biedma 883, T011-4330 0800, www.cicerones.org.ar. Non-profit organization offering volunteer greeting/guiding service for visitors to the city. Free, safe and different.
Class Adventure Travel, JA Cabrera 4423/29, C1414, T011-4833 8400, USA T1-877-240 4770 (Toll Free), UK T020-7096 1259, international T001-512 535 2536, www.cat- travel.com. Dutch-owned and run, with 10 years of experience. Excellent for tailor-made travel solutions throughout the continent. CAT has offices in several South American countries.
Cultour, www.cultour.com.ar. A highly recommended walking tour of the city, 3-4 hrs led by a group of charming Argentine history/tourism graduates. In English and Spanish.
Ecole del Sur Travel, Av Rivadavia 1479, p 1B, T011- 4383 1026, www.ecoledelsur.com. Organizes tours, packages and accommodation.
Eternautas, Av Julio A Roca 584, p 7, T011-5031 9916/15 4173 1078, www.eternautas.

com. Historical, cultural and artistic tours of the city and Pampas guided in English, French or Spanish by historians and other social scientists from the University of Buenos Aires. Flexible and highly recommended.

Eves Turismo, Tucumán 702, T011-4393 6151, www.eves.com. Helpful and efficient, recommended for flights.

Exprinter, Sáenz Peña 615, p 7 office 101, T011-4393 4160, Galería Güemes, www.exprinterviajes.com.ar. Especially their 5-day, 4-night tour to Iguazú and San Ignacio Miní.

Flyer, Reconquista 617, p 8, T011-4313 8224, www.flyer.com.ar. English, Dutch, German spoken. Recommended, especially for *estancias*, fishing, polo and motor-home rental.

HI Travel Argentina, Florida 835, T011-4511 8723, www.hitravel.com.ar.

Nomads Community Travel Agency, Lima 11, CP1073, T011-5218 3059, www.comunidadnomade.com.ar. Tailor-made trips around Buenos Aires, the surrounding area and throughout Argentina.

Pride Travel, Paraguay 523 p 2, T011- 5218 6556, www.pride-travel.com. The best choice for gay and lesbian travellers in Argentina; they also rent apartments.

Say Hueque, Viamonte 749, p 6, of 1, T011-5199 2517/20, and in Palermo at Guatemala 4845, p1 of 4, T011-4775 7862, www.sayhueque.com. Good-value tours for independent travellers in Argentina. Friendly, English-speaking staff. Specializes in trips to Patagonia, Iguazú and Mendoza.

Tangol, Florida 971, ground floor, local 31, T011-4312 7276, www.tangol.com. Friendly, independent travel agency specializing in football and tango. Also offers city tours, various sports, such as polo and paragliding, trips to ranches, plane and bus tickets, and accommodation. Overland trips to Patagonia, Sep-Apr. English spoken. Special deals for students. A reliable and dynamic company. Recommended.

Transhumans Voyages, Av Córdoba 966, T011-1567 316591, www.transhumans voyages.info. A great company that promotes responsible tourism. They organize trips to the Northeast, Northwest, around Buenos Aires and in Patagonia based on cultural experiences and respecting the environment. A portion of the cost of your holiday goes toward environmental education in schools in rural Argentina. Highly recommended.

Transport

Air
For airport details, see page 6; for flight details, see page 7.

Ezeiza has 2 terminals: 'A' for all airlines except **Aerolíneas Argentinas**, which uses 'B'. 'A' has a very modern check-in hall. There are duty free shops (expensive), exchange facilities (**Banco de la Nación**; **Banco Piano**; **Global Exchange**) and ATMs (Visa and MasterCard), post office (open 0800-2000), Secure Bag US$10, and a left luggage office (US$2 per piece). There is a **Devolución IVA/Tax Free** desk (return of VAT). *Locutorios* with limited internet access. For more information see www.aa2000.com.ar.

Aeroparque terminal is divided into 2 sections, 'A' for all arrivals and **Aerolíneas Argentinas** and LAN check-in desks, 'B' for **Puna** and **LADE** check-in desks. On the 1st floor there is a *patio de comidas* (a food court), several shops and the airport tax counter. At the airport you'll find tourist information, car rental, bus companies, bank, ATMs, exchange facilities, post office, public phones, Secure Bag (US$10 per piece) and luggage deposit (between sections A-B at the information point), US$4 per piece a day. For more information see www.aa2000.com.ar.

Airport bus
There is an airport bus service run by **Manuel Tienda León**, Av Madero 1299 and San Martín, behind Sheraton Hotel in Retiro,

T011-4315 5115, www.tiendaleon.com.
Buses run to **Ezeiza**: 0400, 0500, every 30 mins from 0600-2100, then 2200 and 2230 (try to be 15 mins early), US$11.50, 50-min journey, and then onto the domestic airport Aeroparque, US$4.50, another 25 mins. **Manuel Tienda León** buses to **Aeroparque** leave every hr from 0710-0255, 20-mins, US$4.50. They can also organize transfers to Mar del Plata, Santa Fe, La Plata and Rosario, from both airports. You can buy your ticket online or at the airport.

Airline offices
Aerolíneas Argentinas (AR) and **Austral**, Perú 2, Av Leandro N Alem 1134 and Av Cabildo 2900, T0810-2228 6527. **Air France-KLM**, San Martín 344 p 23, T011-4317 4700. **Alitalia**, Suipacha 1111, T011-4310 9999. **American Airlines**, Av Santa Fe 881, T011-4318 1111, Av Pueyrredón 1997 and branches in Belgrano and Acassuso. **Avianca**, Carlos Pellegrini 1163 p 4, T011-4394 5990. **British Airways**, Viamonte 570, T011-4320 6600. **Copa**, Carlos Pellegrini 989 p 2, T0810-222 2672. **Cubana**, Sarmiento 552 p 11, T011-4325 0691. **Delta**, Reconquista 737, T0800-666 0133. **Iberia**, Carlos Pellegrini, 1163, T011-4131 1000. **LAB**, Carlos Pellegrini 141, T011-4323 1900. **Lan Chile**, Cerrito 886 and Paraguay, T0810-999 9526. **Líneas Aéreas del Estado (LADE)**, Perú 710, T011-5129 9000, Aeroparque T011-4514 1524. **Lufthansa**, M T Alvear 590, p 6, T011-4319 0600. **Malaysia Airlines**, Suipacha 1111 p 14, T011-431 26971. **Mexicana**, Av Córdoba 1131. **Puna**, Florida 1, T011-4342 7000. **TAM**, Cerrito 1030, T011-4819 4800. **United Airlines**, Av Madero 900, T0810-777 8648. **Varig**, Av Córdoba 972, p 4, T011-4329 9211.

Road
Bus
When leaving Buenos Aires by bus it is best to visit the terminal the day before to buy your ticket and familiarize yourself with the area and where the platforms are, so when you return laden with luggage you know exactly where to go. To get to the bus station, take a Radio Taxi, catch a local bus (nearly all of them stop at the train station nearby), or take the *Subte* Line C and follow the signs to the bus station (not recommended late at night or early in the morning).

Note that buses get heavily booked up Dec-Mar, especially at weekends. All long-distance buses arrive at the Retiro bus terminal at Ramos Mejía and Av Antártida Argentina. For Retiro terminal enquiries, T011-4310 0700. Long-distance bus tickets can now be booked by telephone or through the internet using a credit card.

The biggest bus companies are: **Andesmar**, T011-4313 3717, www.andesmar.com; **Chevallier**, T011-4000 5255, www.nuevachevallier.com.ar; **Flecha Bus** T011-4000 5200, www.flechabus.com.ar; **Vía Bariloche** T011-4315 7700, www.via bariloche.com.ar. A great site to help you plan your journey is www.plataforma10.com. You can check bus prices and times, and can also book tickets for buses all over Argentina.

The terminal is on 3 floors. Departures are displayed on screens. Ticket offices are on the upper floor, but there are hundreds of them so you'll need to consult the list of companies and their office numbers at the top of the escalator. They're organized by regions of the country, and each region is colour-coded. There are left-luggage lockers, requiring tokens from kiosks, US$2.50. Large baggage should be left at *guarda equipaje* on the lower floor. The service of luggage porters is supposed to be free. **Buenos Aires city tourist information** is at desk 83 on the upper floor. Bus information is at the Ramos Mejía entrance on the middle floor.

Car hire
Avis, Cerrito 1527, T011-4326 5542, www.avis.com.ar; **Budget**, San Martín 1225,

T011-4314 7773, www.budget.com.ar, ISIC and GO 25 discount; **Hertz**, Paraguay 1138, T011-4816 8001, www.hertzargentina.com.ar.

Taxis

Pidalo: T011-4956 1200; **Radio Taxi Sur**, T011-4638 2000; **Radio Taxi 5 Minutos**, T011-4523 1200; **Radio Taxi Diez**, T011-4585 5007; **Radio Taxi Premium**, T011-4374 6666.

Sea

The *Buenos Aires Herald* (English-language daily) notes all shipping movements.

Ferry

To **Montevideo** and **Colonia del Sacramento** from Terminal Dársena Norte, Av Antártida Argentina 821 (2 blocks from Av Córdoba and Alem), **Buquebus**, T011-4316 6500, www.buquebus.com (tickets from Terminal or from offices at Av Córdoba 879 and Posadas 1452). Direct to **Montevideo**, 1-4 a day, 3 hrs, US$82 tourist class (return, vehicles US$88, motorcycles US$68, bus connection to Punta del Este US$11 extra).

To Uruguay   As Colonia is in Uruguay and you will need to exit Argentina before you board the ferry. To **Colonia**, services by 2 companies, **Buquebus**, 2-3 ferry services a day, 3 hrs, US$51 return, with bus connection to Montevideo (US$10 extra), motorcycles US$25, cars US$41. **Ferrylíneas Sea Cat** www.seacatcolonia.com, operates a cheaper fast service to Colonia from the same terminal, 1-3 daily, 1 hr, US$53 tourist class (return), vehicles US$61, motorcycles US$36 with bus connection to Punta del Este (US$9 extra). There is a new company called **Colonia Express**, www.coloniaexpress.com, which also runs cheaper trips to Uruguay. They leave from a bit further along the port, offer competitive rates and have a much smaller, slightly faster boat, US$40 return. Their cheapest deals are on Wed. Catch a taxi from town (US$5). Don't forget your passport.

Rail

There are 4 main terminals: **Retiro** (3 lines: Mitre, Belgrano, San Martín in separate buildings), **Constitución**, **Once**, **Federico Lacroze**.

Almost the only passenger trains in Argentina today are Buenos Aires commuter trains, and locals feel they're in pretty bad condition, with the exception of the semi-decent Mitre line to Tigre. There are only a few long-distance services, all very shoddy, and not to be considered as a serious alternative to long-distance bus or air travel.

Tickets are checked before boarding and on the train, and are collected at the end of the journey (so don't lose your ticket!); urban and suburban fares are charged according different sections of each line. For information contact the companies directly: **Ferrobaires**, T011-4304 0028, www.ferrobaires.gba.gov.ar; **Ferrovías**, T011- 4511 8833; **Metropolitano**, T0800-1223 58736, www.metropolitano. com.ar; **Metrovías**, T011-4555 1616, www.metrovias.com.ar; **TBA**, T011-4317 4407, www.tbanet.com.ar; **Trenes Especiales**, T011-4551 1634.

Retiro

Retiro station runs 3 different lines in separate buildings: train information T011-4311 8704. **Mitre line**   Run by TBA, services to all the suburbs, though you're most likely to use it to get to Tigre if you want an alternative to the tourist Tren de la Costa. Urban and suburban services to **Belgrano**, **Mitre** (connection to Tren de la Costa, see below), **Olivos**, **San Isidro**, **Tigre** (see below), **Capilla del Señor** (connection at Victoria, US$1), **Escobar** and **Zárate** (connection at Villa Ballester, US$1). Long-distance services to **Rosario Norte**, 1 weekly on Fri evening, 6 hrs, US$10.50 (return); to **Tucumán** via Rosario, Mon and Fri, 2100, returning Mon and Thu 1000, 26 hrs, US$33.50 sleeper,

US$18 pullman, US$11.50 1st (service run by **NOA Ferrocarriles**, T011-4893 2244).

Belgrano line For trains to the northwestern suburbs (Villa Rosa), run by **Ferrovías**, T011-4511 8833.

San Martín line Run by **Metropolitano**. Urban and suburban services to **Palermo**, **Chacarita**, **Devoto**, **Hurlingham** and **Pilar**. Long-distance services to **Junín**, daily, 5 hrs, US$4.50.

Constitución

Train information T011-4304 0028. Like the terminals of Retiro, it is best not to hang around Constitución longer than you need to. Train and bus stations are favourites of scam artists and pickpockets.

Roca line Run by **Metropolitano**, see above). Urban and suburban services to **La Plata**, US$1.20; **Ezeiza** (the suburb NOT the airport), US$0.35; **Ranelagh**, US$0.27; and **Quilmes**, US$0.20. Long-distance services (run by **Ferrobaires**, T011-4304 0028/3165): to **Bahía Blanca**, 5 weekly, 12½ hrs, US$14; to **Mar del Plata** daily in summer, book ahead, 5 hrs US$12; to **Pinamar**, 2 weekly, 6 hrs US$7; to **Miramar**, in summer only, daily, 7 hrs, US$7; to **Tandil**, weekly, 7½ hrs, US$8; to **Quequén**, 2 weekly, 12 hrs, US$7-13.

Federico Lacroze Urquiza

Train line information, and **Metro headquarters**, run by **Metrovías**, T0800-555 1616 or T011-4555 1616, www.metrovias.com.ar. Suburban services to General Lemos, and long-distance services to Posadas, run by **Trenes Especiales**.

Once

Train information, T011-4861 0043. **Once** train station is notorious for petty crime. Best to avoid it if you can.

Once Sarmiento line Run by **TBA**, see above. Urban and suburban services to **Caballito**; **Flores**; **Merlo**; **Luján** (connection at Moreno) US$0.60;

Mercedes, US$1.20; and **Lobos**. Long-distance services to **Santa Rosa** and **General Pico** can be seasonally interrupted by floods. A fast service runs daily between **Puerto Madero** (station at Av Alicia Moreau de Justo and Perón) and **Castelar**.

Banks

ATMs are widespread throughout the city. Note that most tourists find they have a limit of US$300 a day, and that they need to take this out in 3 US$100 transactions from the ATM. This has nothing to do with your bank, it is a limit that Argentine banks impose (look for **Link** ATMs as they are most reliable). Don't contact your bank about this, they have no control over it. The financial district lies within a small area north of Plaza de Mayo, between Rivadavia, 25 de Mayo, Av Corrientes and Florida. In non-central areas you'll find banks/ATMs along the main avenues. Banks are open Mon-Fri 1000-1500. Most banks charge commission especially on TCs (as much as US$10). US dollar bills are often scanned electronically for forgeries.

American Express offices are at Arenales 707 and Maipú, by Plaza San Martín, T011-4310 3000 or T0810-555 2639, www.americanexpress.com, where you can apply for a card, get financial services and change Amex TCs (1000-1500 only, T0810-444 2437, no commission into US$ or pesos). No commission either at **Banco de la Provincia de Buenos Aires**, several branches, or at **Banco Columbia**, Perón 350. **Citibank**, B Mitre 502, T0810-444 2484, changes only Citicorps TCs, no commission, branch at Florida 199. **General MasterCard office**, Perú 151, T011-4348 7000, www.mastercard.com.ar, 0930-1800. **Visa**, Corrientes 1437 p 2, T011-4379 3400, www.visa.com.ar. Currency exchange *Casas de cambio* include **Banco Piano**, San Martín 345, T011-4321 9200 (has exchange facility at Ezeiza airport, 0500-2400), www.banco piano.com.ar, changes all TCs (commission 2%); **Eves**, Tucumán 702; **Forex**, Marcelo T de Alvear 540, T011-4311 5543; **Banco Ciudad** at Av Córdoba 675 branch is open to tourists (providing passport) for exchange currency and TCs, Mon 1000-1800, Tue-Fri 1000-1700, Sat-Sun 1100-1800. Lost or stolen cards **MasterCard**, T0800-555 0507; **Visa** T011-4379 3333 (T0810-666 3368, from outside BA). Money transfers **Western Union** branches in *Correo Argentino* post offices (for transfers within Argentina) and at Av Córdoba 975 (for all transfers), T0800-800 3030.

Cultural centres

Alliance Française, Córdoba 946, T011-4322 0068, www.alianzafrancesa.org.ar, French library, temporary film and art exhibitions; **Biblioteca Centro Lincoln**, Maipú 672, T011-5382 1536, www.bcl.edu.ar, Mon-Wed 1000-2000, Thu and Fri 1000-1800 (Jan and Feb Mon-Fri 1300-1900), library (borrowing for members only), English/US newspapers; **British Arts Centre** (BAC), Suipacha 1333, T011-4393 6941, www.britishartscentre. org.ar, English plays and films, music concerts and photography exhibitions (closed Jan); **British Council**, Marcelo T. de Alvear 590, p 4, T011-4311 9814, Mon-Thu 0830-1700, Fri 0830-1330; **Goethe Institut**, Corrientes 319/43, T011-4311 8964, German library, Mon, Tue, Thu 1230-1930, Fri 1230-1600, closed Jan, newspapers, free German films shown, cultural programmes, German-language courses, in the same building, upstairs, is the German Club, Corrientes 327; **Instituto Cultural Argentino Norteamericano (ICANA)**, Maipú 672, T011-5382 1500, www.icana.org.ar.

Embassies and consulates

All open Mon-Fri unless stated otherwise. **Australia**, Villanueva 1400 and Zabala, T011-4779 3500, www.argentina.embassy. gov.au, daily 0830-1100, ticket queuing system, take bus 29 along Av Luis María Campos to Zabala; **Belgium**, Defensa 113 p 8, T011-4331 0066, 0800-1300, www.diplomatie.be/buenosaires/; **Bolivia**, Consulate, Alsina 1886, T011-4381 4171, www.embajadade bolivia. com.ar, 0830-1530, visa while you wait or a month wait (depending on the country of origin), tourist bureau; **Brazil**, Consulate, Pellegrini 1363, p 5, T011-4515 6500, www.conbrasil. org.ar, 1000-1300, tourist visa takes at least 48 hrs, US$100; **Canada**, Tagle 2828, T011-4808 1000, www.canadainternational. gc.ca/argentina-argentine, Mon-Thu 0830-1230, 1330-1730, tourist visa Mon-Thu 0845-1130; **Chile**, Consulate, San Martín 439, p 9, T011-4394 6582, www.embajadadechile.com.ar/embajada. asp, 0900-1330; **Denmark**, Consulate, Alem 1074, p 9, T011-4312 6901, www.dinamarca.net, Mon-Thu 0930-1200; **France**, Santa Fe 846, p 4, T011-4312 2409, www.consulatfrance.int.ar, 0900-1230, 1400-1600 (by appointment); **Germany**, Villanueva 1055, T011-4778 2500, www.embajada-alemana.org.ar, 0830-1100; **Ireland**, Av Del Libertador 1068 p 6, T011-5787 0801, www.embassyof ireland.org.ar, 0900-1300, 1400-1530; **Italy**, consulate at Marcelo T de Alvear 1125/49, T011-4816 6133/36, www.consbuenosaires. esteri.it, Mon, Tue, Thu, Fri 0800-1100; **Netherlands**, Olga Cossentini 831 p 3, Puerto Madero, T011- 4338 0050, www.embajadaholanda.int.ar, Mon-Thu 0900-1300, Fri 0900-1230; **New Zealand**, Pellegrini 1427 p 5, I0I1-4328 0747, www.nzembassy.com/argentina, Mon-Thu 0900-1300, 1400-1730, Fri 0900-1300; **Norway**, Esmeralda 909, p 3 B, T011-4312 2204, www.noruega.org.ar, 0930-1400; **Spain**, Consulate, Guido 1760, T011-4811 0070, www.mae.es/consulados/buenosaires, 0815-1430; **Sweden**, Tacuarí 147 p 6, T011-4329 0800, www.swedenabroad.com/

buenosaires, 1000-1200; **Switzerland**, Santa Fe 846, p10, T011-4311 6491, www.eda.admin.ch/buenosaires, 0900-1200; **UK**, Luis Agote 2412 (near corner Pueyrredón and Guido), T011-4808 2200 (call T011-15-5114 1036, for emergencies only out of normal office hours), http://ukin argentina.fco.gov.uk/en/, 0900-1300 (Jan-Feb 0900-1200); **Uruguay**, Consulate, Av Las Heras 1907, T011-4807 3045, www.embajadadeluruguay. com.ar, 0930-1730, visa takes up to 72 hrs; **US Embassy and Consulate General**, Colombia 4300, T011-5777 4533 (for emergencies involving US citizens, call T011-5777 4354 or T011-5777 4873 after office hours), http://argentina.usembassy.gov/.

_____

Emergencies
Central Police Station: Moreno 1550, Virrey Cevallos 362, T011-4370 5911/5800 (emergency, T101 from any phone, free). See page 19for **Comisaría del Turista** (tourist police).

_____

Internet
Prices range from US$0.50-US$1.50 per hr, shop around. Most _locutorios_ (phone offices) have internet access.

_____

Language schools
There are many good Spanish teachers and schools, for advice contact South American Explorers, www.saexplorers.org, for their recommendations.

Private teachers
Cristina Gioveni, T011-156 859 3434, www. sffi.com.ar, or cristinagioveni@yahoo.com.ar, lessons either at her office or at the your place, group and 1-to-1 lessons available and take a taster class for free; **Ezequiel Cerioni**, www.bahabla.com, ezequielcerioni@ gmail.com, qualified, will visit your house or you can go to his, is entertaining and often recommended; **Gisela Giunti**, J.E. Uriburu 541, 6th Floor 'A', T011-155 626 0162, www.giselagiunti.com, offers personalized, private classes for individuals or small groups, competitive rates, great reviews and highly recommended.

Schools
Academia Buenos Aires, Hipólito Yrigoyen 571, 4th floor, T011-4345 5954, www.academiabuenosaires.com, slightly more expensive classes than most, but high attention to detail and great teachers, also offers a recommended school in Montevideo, Uruguay, www.academiauruguay.com; **All-Spanish**, Talcahuano 77, p 1, T011- 4381 3914, www.all-spanish.com.ar, good reports; **Amauta Spanish School**, Frederico Lacroze 2129, T011-4777 2130, www.amautaspanishschool.org, individual lessons or small groups, also has a school in Bariloche; **Argentina I.L.E.E**, T011- 4782 7173, www.argentinailee.com, recommended by individuals and organizations alike, also have schools in Córdoba and Bariloche; **Ecole del SurTravel**, Av Rivadavia 1479, p 1, department B, T011-4383 1026, www.ecoledelsur.com. A language school that also organizes tours, packages and accommodation. **Elebaires**, Av de Mayo 1370, office 10, 3rd floor, T011-4371 3149, www.elebaires.com.ar, small school with focused classes, also offers 1-to-1 lessons and excursions, recommended; **Español Andando**, T011-5278 9886, www.espanol-andando.com, offers a different approach to classes, recommended, courses run for a week, and each day you will meet your fellow students and your teacher in a different part of the city and learn how the locals say it; **Expanish**, Viamonte 927, 1st floor, T011-4322 0011, www.expanish.com, well-organized Spanish courses which can involve excursions, accommodation and Spanish lessons in sister schools in Lima, Peru and Chile, highly recommended; **IBL (International Bureau of Language)**, Florida 165, 3rd floor, T011-4331 4250, www.ibl.com.ar, group and

1-to-1 lessons, all levels; **Universidad de Buenos Aires**, 25 de Mayo 221, T011- 4334 7512, www.idiomas.filo.uba.ar, offers cheap, coherent courses, including summer intensive courses.

Medical services
Urgent medical service For free municipal ambulance service to an emergency hospital department (day and night) **Casualty ward**, **Sala de guardia**, T107, or T011-4923 1051/58 (SAME).

Inoculations If not provided, buy the vaccines in **Laboratorio Biol**, Uriburu 153, T011-4953 7215, or in larger chemists. Many chemists have signs indicating that they give injections and any hospital with an infectology department will give hepatitis A. **Dirección de Sanidad de Fronteras y Terminales de Transporte**, Ing Huergo 690, T011-4343 1190, Mon 1400-1500, Tue-Wed 1100-1200, Thu and Fri 1600-1700 (bus 20 from Retiro), no appointment required, yellow fever only, take passport; **Hospital Rivadavia**, Av Las Heras 2670, T011-4809 2000, Mon-Fri, 0700-1300 (bus 10, 37, 59, 60, 62, 92, 93 or 102 from Plaza Constitución); **Travel Medicine Service (Centros Médicos Stamboulian)**, 25 de Mayo 464, T011-4311 3000, French 3085, T011-5236 7772, also in Belgrano and Flores, private health advice for travellers and inoculations centre.

Public hospital **British Hospital**, Perdriel 74, T011-4309 6400, www.hospitalbritanico. org.ar, US$42 a visit, first-aid centre (*centros asistenciales*); **German Hospital**, Av Pueyrredón 1640, between Beruti and Juncal, T011-4827 7000, www.hospitalale man.com.ar, first-aid centre; **Hospital Argerich**, Almte Brown corner of Pi and

Margall 750, T011-4121 0700; **Hospital Juan A Fernández**, Cerviño and Bulnes, T011-4808 2600, good medical attention.

Dental treatment **Carroll Forest**, Vuelta de Obligado 1551 (Belgrano), T011-4781 9037, info@carroll-forest.com.ar, excellent dental treatment centre; **Dental Argentina**, T011-4828 0821, www.dental-argentina.com.ar.

Post offices
Correo Central, **Correos Argentinos**, Sarmiento and Alem, T011-4891 9191, www.correoargentino.com.ar, Mon-Fri, 0800-2000, Sat 1000-1300, poste restante (only to/from domestic destinations) on ground floor (US$0.90 per letter), philatelic section Mon-Fri 1000-1700, T011- 5550 5176; **Centro Postal Internacional**, for all parcels over 2 kg for mailing internationally, at Av Comodoro Py and Antártida Argentina, near Retiro station, helpful, many languages spoken, packaging materials available, Mon-Fri 1000-1700; **DHL**, T0810-222 2345, www.dhl.com.ar; **FedEx**, T0810-333 3339, www.fedex.com; **Post office**, Montevideo 1408 near Plaza V López, also at Santa Fe 945 and many others, friendly staff, Spanish only; **UPS**, T0800-222 2877, www.ups.com.

Telephone
International and local calls, internet and fax from phone offices (*locutorios* or *telecentros*), of which there are many in the city centre. For more information, see Essentials A-Z, page 23.

Visas
Migraciones: (Immigration), Antártida Argentina 1355, edificio 4, T011-4317 0200, daily 0730-1330, www.migraciones.gov.ar (visas extended mornings only). See also Essentials, page 23.

Around Buenos Aires

If you don't relish the frenzy of a big city, especially at the end of a trip exploring some of the widest landscapes on earth, you'll be relieved to know there are calm rural estancias (cattle farms), the fascinating Tigre river delta, and cowboy towns which celebrate an authentic gaucho culture – all within an hour or two of Buenos Aires.

Ins and outs

Mataderos is on the western edge of the city, and worth visiting only on Sundays, when it's the site of a wonderful market, with displays of gaucho horsemanship. The air is filled with the smoky aroma of grilling steak on *asados*, and there's even tango dancing. If gaucho culture intrigues you, it's worth setting out for the impeccably preserved 1900s gaucho towns of San Antonio de Areco, to the west of the city, or Chascomus in the south (handy for Ezeiza International Airport). There are lots of grand estancias near both towns, where you can try horse riding or simply lap up the luxury. Details on these places are in the next chapter, Buenos Aires Province.

Closer at hand, the two most popular destinations for day trips are north of the city along the coast of the Río de la Plata, easily reached by train from the city. San Isidro is a beautiful old colonial suburb where you can find huge luxury residential mansions, a wonderful church on the plaza and a ring of smart shops in the charming old quarter, making it a pleasant place to stroll around, especially at weekends when the craft market is on. Also appealing is the Tigre river delta which is a maze of overgrown waterways that can be explored by boat or local ferry. Find a waterfont restaurant, or a romantic boutique hotel on stilts hidden away up a lazy river and spend a few days relaxing.

Finally, you could take a boat trip across the Río de la Plata to the quaint Portuguese colonial town of Colonia del Sacramento (which is in Uruguay). Stroll around the antique buildings on this quiet peninsula, or hire a bike: there's nothing much to do here except eat and gaze at the views, but the architecture is very appealing and there's an amazing sense of calm. After the constant bustle of Buenos Aires, Colonia is a welcome retreat. ▸▸ For listings, see pages 81-87.

Mataderos

On the western edge of the city in an area where historically cattle were slaughtered, there is now a popular market, the **Feria de Mataderos** ⓘ *Lisandro de la Torre and Av de los Corrales, www.feriademataderos.com.ar, every Sun and holidays from 1100, Sat 1800-2400 in summer.* Take *Subte* E to the end of the line and then a taxi (US$4), or if there's a group of you, take buses 36, 92, 97, 126, 141. A Radio Taxi all the way will cost US$12. It's a long way out of the centre (about two hours by bus), but worth it to see this fair of Argentine handicrafts and traditional artwork, with music and dance festivals, demonstrations of gaucho horsemanship skills, typical regional food, and games such as *pato*, a game played on horseback, originally with a duck, and *carrera de sortijas* where players on horseback have to spear a ring on a string with their lance. Nearby is the **Museo de los Corrales** ⓘ *Av de los Corrales 6436, T011-4687 1949, Sun 1300-1900.*

San Isidro → *For listings, see pages 81-87.*

Just to the north of Buenos Aires city, 22 km away, San Isidro is an attractive small town with a lovely setting on the coast, easily reached by the **Tren de La Costa** (see below) or local train from Retiro, Mitre station (US$0.75). It's an appealing place to come for an afternoon, for a stroll along the historical old quarter by the river, or to shop in the converted old railway station. This is the most sought-after residential area in greater

Buenos Aires, and there are lots of bars and places to eat along the coast, with pretty green spaces for walking or relaxing. The **tourist information office** ⓘ *just off the central plaza Mitre, at Ituzaingo 608, on the corner with Av del Libertador, T011-4512 3209, www.sanisidro.gov.ar*, is staffed by extremely helpful bilingual staff.

Start your tour of San Isidro at the Tren de la Costa train station, nicely renovated, and now housing shops where you can pick up good handicrafts as well as clothes and accessories. Walk up into the pretty main **Plaza Mitre**, filled with shady mature trees and fragrant flowers in summer, and where there is a handicrafts market every weekend. From here, have a look at the old Municipal buildings, before walking along Beccar Varela Street to look at the aristocratic houses. This was historically the site of country houses for the aristocracy in the late 19th century, and there are a number of fine colonial buildings including several country houses (*quintas*). **Quinta Pueyrredón** houses the Museo **Pueyrredón**, containing artefacts from the life of General Juan Martín Pueyrredón. The main shopping street, with lots of *locutorios* and places you can download and print photos, as well as conventional shops, is **Belgrano**, between Avenida del Libertador and Avenida Centenario, the busy main road into Buenos Aires city.

The **Ribera**, the area by the coast stretching southeast of the centre, is green and peaceful, with plenty of park areas where you can sit gazing out at the great view of the Río de la Plata. There are marinas for yachts and windsurfing, and the **Club Náutico San Isidro**, reached from Mitre. There are also plenty of places to eat along here as this is a popular upmarket nightspot for *Porteños*, all along the coast road southeast of the centre of San Isidro from Primera Junta southeast to Paraná. It's worth strolling onto the viewpoint from the Mirador de Roque Sáenz Peña for the views over to Buenos Aires. Further southeast, there's a small nature reserve right on the Río de la Plata, the **Reserva Ecológica Municipal**, *T011-4747 6179, 0900-1900, guided visit at 1700 in summer; 0900-1800, guided visits Sat-Sun 1600 in winter, free entry*, which hosts an impressive array of birdlife, with over 200 species. Access is from the coast road, Camino de la Ribera, via Vicente López.

An interesting country house to visit is the French-inspired **Villa Ocampo** ⓘ *T011-4807 4428, Thu-Sun 1230-1800, US$3, students US$2*. Built in 1891, this beautiful house with galleried verandas and attractive gardens was the home of the famous Argentine writer Victoria Ocampo, where she frequently entertained illustrious visitors from Argentina's literary world. Take a taxi as this is 10 blocks north of the centre. Ask the tourist office for precise directions.

San Isidro is most famous for the **Hipódromo San Isidro**, its magnificent turf racecourse. Built in 1935, this immense racecourse is one of the best known in South America. Races are run every Wednesday, and some Saturdays or Sundays from 1500-2000. Beyond the compact town centre, the residential area is huge and sprawling, and is *the* place to live if you're a wealthy *Porteño*. Naturally, nearby is where you find Argentina's biggest shopping mall, the disarmingly immense **Unicenter Shopping**, at Paraná and the Ruta Panamericana, see page 66. Don't even attempt to get there by bus: take a taxi, ask the driver to collect you at a predetermined time and allow at least half a day. All the main brands are here, as well as a good range of restaurants in the Patio de Comidas.

Tren de la Costa → _T011-4002 6000._

One of Argentina's most comfortable trains is this tourist service that whisks visitors from Maipú station in the Vicente López area of Buenos Aires all the way to Tigre, via some of the most picturesque spots on the coast of the Río de la Plata. To get to Maipú, take a normal (TBA) commuter train from Retiro in the centre of Buenos Aires and change at Maipú for the Tren de la Costa. San Isidro is the most appealing place to stop on your way to Tigre, but you could also try Borges station, for the pleasant residential area of Olivos, with its waterfront filled with millionaires' homes, and Barrancas, where you can hire rollerblades and bikes, and visit the second-hand market. You can get off and on as many times as you like for the fixed single ticket price of US$2.10. Trains leave every 20 minutes, Monday to Thursday 0710-2300, Friday 0710-2400, Saturday and Sunday 0830-0010. Buses to Tren de la Costa are No 60 from Constitución, Nos 19 or 71 from Once, and No 152 from the centre. For those on a tight budget, you can also reach Tigre by taking the TBA train all the way from Retiro for US$0.45 (55 minutes). Trains leave every seven minutes Monday to Friday, or every 15 minutes Saturday and Sunday. It takes 35 minutes to reach San Isidro from Maipú, and 60 minutes to reach Tigre.

Tigre → _For listings, see pages 81-87._

Tigre is deservedly the city's most popular weekend destination: a town based on the edge of the magnificent river delta of the Río Paraná, some 32 km northwest of the city. The delta is a maze of waterways and hundreds of islands, formed by the accumulation of sediment brought down by the mighty Paraná river that runs from the border with Brazil down to the Río de la Plata, slicing between the First and Second sections of the delta. The delta is a natural paradise, mostly wild and untouched, the lush, jungly banks of the islands making picturesque settings for quaint wooden holiday homes on stilts, the odd boutique hotel, and restaurants hidden miles away from the noise of the city and reached only by boat. In fact, some 3000 people live on the delta islands, and since there are no paths or bridges, the only way to get around is by boat, which is how services such as supermarkets, banks and libraries are brought to the islanders. Tigre is the perfect place to cool down on a hot afternoon in summer, and even if you only come for a few hours, you can take one of the regular motor launches for a 60- or 90-minute tour of the nearby rivers for a pleasurable introduction to this watery world. If a tour isn't your thing, just catch the local 1920s-style wooden ferries to a point along the river to explore. Most people stop at Tres Bocas (45 minutes each way), as there are three restaurants to choose from. A return journey will cost around US$4: just wait at the little wharf until a boat comes past – every 10 minutes or so – and wave until they see you. With more time, hire a kayak to see the wonderfully overgrown expanses at more leisure, or try rowing or canoeing. There are many houses you can rent by the night on the islands (from around US$45, 20% more at weekends), reached by the regular motor launch bus service and visited by a mobile food shop. You could hide away here for a night or two on a romantic retreat; it's a peaceful place to escape to. All houses have electricity and phone, but bring drinking water and sunscreen.

There are lots of restaurants scattered throughout the delta, and also _recreos_ – little resorts with facilities such as swimming pools and tennis courts, as well as waterfront bars and restaurants. One of these is **El Alcazar**, just 10 minutes' boat journey from Tigre, with tennis and volleyball, by a sandy beach, where you can bring your own steaks to barbecue on the *parrilla* grills. Tigre itself has a funfair and an excellent fruit and handicrafts market; a short walk from the centre, along Mitre and turn right at the Delta station. The amusement park, **Parque de Diversiones** ① *Fri-Sun only*, is immediately on your left, with the Casino next door in a soulless concrete building. The fruit market, **Puerto de Frutos** ① *daily 1100-2000*, is four blocks further along on the left, on Sarmiento. There's a fairly drab town centre with everything you might need, but the riverside area is the most picturesque, and here you'll find one excellent hotel, **Villa Julia**, which also serves superb food (see Sleeping, page 83). Tigre is a great place to visit any time of the year, with a mild climate even in winter, but note that it's quietest midweek: in summer it gets very busy at weekends, though the festive atmosphere is very appealing in itself. Regattas are held in November and March. Remember to bring a hat and insect repellent in summer.

Tigre can be reached by bus from Constitución (bus No 60): the 60 'bajo' takes a little longer than the 60 'alto' but is more interesting for sightseeing. Tigre is also easily reached on the Tren de la Costa (see above) and you should get off at Estación Fluvial, not Delta. The direct train from Retiro station, Buenos Aires (TBA Mitre section) terminates at the Tigre station, which is different to that of the Tren de la Costa (it is more central and you can see the ferry terminal from the entrance). The journey takes 60 minutes and costs US$0.75; make sure you stay on the train until it reaches the last stop. Alternatively, you can take the train to Bartolomé Mitre and change at the Maipú station (the stations are linked) for the Tren de la Costa. There is an excellent **tourist office** ① *next to Estación Fluvial, at Mitre 305, www.tigre.gov.ar, T011-4512 4497, daily 1000-1800*, with helpful English-speaking staff who can show you the huge folder of houses to rent by the night (complete with photographs) and advise you of boat/bus times to reach them. There's one excellent hotel in Tigre itself, and some average hotels among the delta islands, with a gorgeous boutique hotel, **La Pascuala** (see Sleeping, page 83) in the Second Section, on the other side of the Río Paraná.

Before you take a boat trip, have a stroll along the riverside, the path parallel to Lavalle that leads to Paseo Victorica. You'll pass several rowing clubs, some of them in palatial old buildings, such as the British Rowing Club of 1873, the Buenos Aires Rowing Club, and the Italian Club, as well as the Tudor-style half-timbered Club Regata opposite. The main tourist centre is around the old railway station, **Estación Fluvial**, the large old building, now tastefully restored, with souvenir shops, a McDonald's, and many companies selling boat trips: **Sturla** ① *T011- 4731 1300*, is one of the most reliable, offering a 90-minute trip for US$7. Boats leave from the quayside by the Estación Fluvial, and you can pick from big catamarans or smaller wooden boats. The tour guides on all boats speak English and give an informative tour.

There's one museum in Tigre, the **Museo Naval de la Nación** ① *Paseo Victoria 602, T011-4749 0608, Mon-Thu 0830-1230, Fri 0800-1730, Sat-Sun 1000-1830, US$0.60*, which covers the origins and development of the Argentine navy, with lots of model ships. There are also relics of the Falklands/Malvinas War on display outside. You might also be interested in the **Municipal Art Gallery** ① *Paseo Victoria 972, T011-4512 4528, museo dearte@tigre.gov.ar, Mon-Fri 0900-1900, Sat-Sun 1200-1900, US$1.50*, a 10-minute walk along the river and housed in the newly restored Tigre Hotel from 1909 – a wonderfully ornate building with many chandeliers. On show are mainly 20th-century works of art detailing the river and its inhabitants. In the delta there is a small museum based around the house of Sarmiento – one of Argentina's most famous presidents. You'll see it from the river, it is a huge glass enclosure with a small wooden house inside like a big fish bowl. You can ask the ferry driver to drop you off there.

Isla Martín García → *For listings, see pages 81-87.*

Situated in the Río de la Plata just off the Uruguayan coast and some 45 km north of Buenos Aires, Martín García is now a provincial nature reserve and one of the best excursions from Buenos Aires, with many trails through the cane brakes, trees and rocky outcrops, and interesting birds and flowers.

This was the site of Juan Díaz de Solís' landfall in 1516, and the island's strategic position has given it a chequered history. It was used for quarantining immigrants from Europe, and then as a prison: four 20th-century Argentine presidents have been detained here, including Juan Perón, and in 1914 British sailors were interned here, as were survivors from the *Graf Spee* in the Second World War. Evidence ranges from stone-quarries used for building the older churches of Buenos Aires to four gun batteries and a *faro* (lighthouse) dating from 1890. The **Museo Histórico** in the former *pulpería* houses a display of artefacts, documents and photos. Wildlife is varied, particularly around the edges of the island, and includes laurels, ceibo and several species of orchid. Over 200 species of birds visit the island. Take insect repellent.

There are four weekly boat trips which run from Tigre at 0900, returning 2030, taking three hours. Prices are around US$47 including a light lunch, *asado* and guide (US$99 per person including weekend overnight at inn, full board). Reservations can be made through Cacciola ① *Florida 520, 1st floor, Office 113, T011-4393 6100, www.cacciolaviajes.com*, who also handle bookings for the inn and restaurant on the island.

Colonia del Sacramento → *For listings, see pages 81-87.*

A Portuguese colonial town on the east bank of the Río de la Plata, Colonia del Sacramento is a very popular destination for excursions from Buenos Aires. The **airport** is 17 km out of town along Route 1; for a taxi to Colonia, buy a ticket in the building next to arrivals, US$2.50. The modern town, with a population of 22,000, which extends along a bay, is charming and lively with neat, leafy streets. The small historic neighbourhood is particularly interesting because there is so much well-preserved colonial architecture. There is a pleasant Plaza 25 de Agosto and a grand Intendencia Municipal (Méndez and Avenida General Flores, the main street). The best beach is Playa Ferrando, 2 km to the east (buses from General Flores every two hours). There are regular sea and air connections with Buenos Aires and a free port. Colonia del Sacramento is in Uruguay. Remember to take your passport with you. There are no transport taxes although you will be subject to immigration formalities if you travel further into Uruguay.

The **tourist office** ① *Flores and Rivera, T+598 (0)52-23700, Mon-Fri 0900-1900, Sat and Sun 0900-1900*, has good maps of the Barrio Histórico. There is also a tourist office at the passenger terminal by the dock.

Sights → *Phone code +598-(0)52.*

With its narrow streets (wander around Calle de los Suspiros), colonial buildings and reconstructed city walls, the Barrio Histórico has been declared Patrimonio Cultural de la Humanidad by UNESCO. The **Plaza Mayor** (Plaza 25 de Mayo) is especially picturesque. At its eastern end is the **Puerta del Campo**, the restored city gate and drawbridge. On the south side is the **Museo Portugués**; see also the narrow Calle de los Suspiros, nearby. At the western end of the Plaza are the **Museo Municipal** in the former house of Almirante Brown (with indigenous archaeology, historical items, palaeontology and natural history), the **Casa Nacarello** next door, the **Casa del Virrey**, and the ruins of the **Convento de San Francisco** (1695), to which is attached the *faro* (lighthouse) built in 1857 (free, but a tip or donation is appreciated). Entry to the museums in this historic quarter is by combined ticket bought from Museo Municipal: US$2.50, opening hours tend to be 1100-1730 every day.

Just north of the Plaza Mayor a narrow street, the Calle Misiones de los Tapes, leads east to the river. At its further end is the tiny **Museo del Azulejo** housed in the Casa Portuguesa. Two blocks north of here is the Calle Playa which runs east to the Plaza Manuel Lobo/Plaza de Armas, on the northern side of which is the **Iglesia Matriz**, on Vasconcellos, the oldest church in Uruguay. Though destroyed and rebuilt several times, the altar dates from the 16th century. Free concerts are held each Friday during the summer months on the church grounds. Two blocks north of the church, on the northern edge of the old city, are the fortifications of the **Bastión del Carmen**; just east of it is the **Teatro Bastión del Carmen**. One block south of the Bastión, at San José and España, is the **Museo Español**, formerly the house of General Mitre. Hire a buggy or a bicycle and explore, then pick a restaurant and peacefully soak up the sun, eat a huge lunch and enjoy a cold drink. Wonderful.

Estancias near Buenos Aires

Many of the province's finest *estancias* can be visited relatively easily from Buenos Aires, either to spend a day (*día de campo*) or longer. *Día de campo* usually includes horse riding, or riding in a horse-drawn carriage over the *estancia*'s lands, followed by lunch. This is usually a traditional *asado*, often cooked outside with half a cow speared over an open fire: quite a spectacle and absolutely delicious. In the afternoon you may be treated to demonstrations of farm life, music and dancing from the region, or you might just choose to walk in the beautiful grounds of the *estancia*, read under a tree or swim in the pool. To really appreciate the luxury or peace of an *estancia*, an overnight stay is recommended. Most places are still run as working farms by their owners, who will welcome you personally, and staying with them gives you a unique insight into Argentine rural life and history. Several good websites with details of *estancias* are: www. turismo.gov.ar, www.caminodelgaucho.com.ar, and www.raturestancias.com.ar.

There are many *estancias* grouped around the attractive towns of **San Antonio de Areco** (see page 91), **Chascomús** (see page 97) and **Dolores** (see page 97), all listed under Buenos Aires Province.

Around Buenos Aires listings

For Sleeping and Eating price codes and other relevant information, see pages 11-17.

● Sleeping

San Isidro *p76*
$$$$ Del Casco, Av Libertador 16, 170, T/F011- 4732 3993, www.hoteldel

casco.com.ar. Perfectly situated gracious colonial-style country house built in 1892, now beautifully converted. The bedrooms are huge and tastefully decorated, with old furniture and luxurious bathrooms. The service, from the young bilingual staff, is excellent, and the breakfasts are enormous.

All highly recommended. A peaceful alternative for exploring the city. **$$$ Posada de San Isidro Apart Hotel**, Maipú 66, T011-4732 1221, www.posadasanisidro. com.ar. Pleasant, modern functional rooms in a new building, offering impeccable and good value self-catering accommodation. Small pool, breakfast available, handy for the main line train station.

Colonia del Sacramento

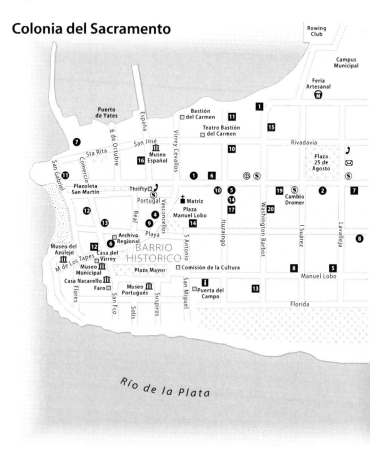

Tigre p82

$$$$ La Pascuala, 'la segunda seccion', 1 hr by motor launch, arrange with reception, T011-4378 0982, www.lapascuala.com. One of Argentina's most delightful places to stay, this is

To Real de San Carlos
To **2**
Cnl Arroyo
Av Gen Artigas
Alberto Méndez
Rivera
Dr D Fosalba
V García
To Playa Ferrando (2 km)
Intendencia
Municipal **i**
18
Plaza de Deportes
i
To Real de San Carlos
3
Av General Flores
18 de Julio
Av F D Roosevelt
To Montevideo
@
S
PUERTO
Punta Car
Europcar
i Thrifty
To Buenos Aires

Eating 🍴
Blanco y Negro **10**
Club Colonia **2**
El Asador **14**
El Drugstore & Viejo Barrio **4**
El Torreón **11**
La Amistad **8**
La Bodeguita **12**
Lo de Renata **1**
Mercosur **5**
Mesón de la Plaza **9**
Pulpería Los Faroles **6**
Yacht Club **7**

an exclusive and intimate boutique hotel hidden far away from civilization in the wild further reaches of the Second Section of the Tigre delta. The hotel consists of 15 individual suite-lodges on stilts, connected by wooden walkways, each with a huge and luxurious bedroom with its own veranda looking over the river, and an immense bathroom, all beautifully designed for maximum calm and relaxation, equipped with everything you could possibly need. The price is high, but all meals, wine and afternoon tea are included, and the service is top notch. Highly recommended.

$$$$ Rumbo 90 Delta Lodge and Spa, in the eastern area of the delta, 45 mins by launch from Tigre, T011-155 843 9454, www.rumbo90.com.ar. In a glorious natural setting, with 40 ha of rainforest to wander around in, this is a comfortable hotel, bedrooms have smart bathrooms with jacuzzi and there is a spa offering facial treatments. Not as luxurious as **La Pascuala**, but a lovely setting.

$$$$ Villa Julia, Paseo Victorica 800, T011-4749 0642, www.villajuliaresort.com.ar. This beautiful villa, built in 1906 on the waterfront, has now been tastefully converted into a chic little boutique hotel with just 9 rooms. There are superb views from the upper rooms, and all are decorated in the original style of the hotel, with very comfortable beds. Many of the bathrooms have the original furniture and pretty art nouveau tiles. The sitting room downstairs is calm and elegant, and the peaceful dining room is a really special place for dinner with a small but imaginative menu. Open to non-residents too.

Hostels

$$$ Marco Polo Náutico, Paraná de las Palmas and Cruz Colorada, T011-4728 0395, www.marcopoloinnnautico.com. A wonderful retreat in the middle of the delta reached by a local ferry. Spacious doubles and triples available. A little pricey but a lovely place to relax for a few days. Kayaking, swimming pool, beach, pool tables and bar.

$ Tigre Hostel, Av del Libertador 190, T011-4749 4034, www.tigrehostel.com.ar. A lovely river house in the heart of Tigre itself, close to shops and the boat station. Stunning double (**$$**) and triple bedrooms, with a cosy living room in which to while away the afternoons. Recommended.

Camping
$$ TAMET Tigre Delta, Río Luján y Abra Vieja, T011-4728 0396, www.tamet.com.ar. Clean, 3-ha park with hot showers, *hostería* doubles with bath also available (including breakfast). Table tennis, volleyball, canoes, restaurant and basic cooking facilities.

Isla Martín García *p84*
$$ Hostería Martín García, owned by Cacciola. US$7 per person for hostel accommodation with private bath. US$6 per person with shared bathroom. For bungalow rental, T0315-24546.

Camping
Martín García, T011-4728 10808.

Colonia del Sacramento *p80, map p82*
$$ Don Antonio Posada, Ituzaingó 232, T+598 (0)52-25344, www.posadadon antonio.com. 1870 building, buffet breakfast, a/c, TV, garden, pool, internet, Wi-Fi, excellent.
$$$ Esperanza, Gral Flores 237, T+598 (0)52-22922, www.hotelesperanzaspa.com. Charming, with sauna, pool and treatments.
$$$ Italiano, Intendente Suárez 105, T+598 (0)52-27878. With or without bath, good restaurant, heated pool. Recommended.
$$$ Plaza Mayor, del Comercio 111, T/F+598 (0)52-23193, www.posadaplazamayor. com/Ingles. Lovely, English spoken.
$$$ Posada de la Flor, Ituzaingó 268, T+598 (0)52-30794, www.posada-delaflor.com. At the quiet end of C Ituzaingó, next to the river and to the Barrio Histórico, simply decorated rooms on a charming patio and roof terrace with river views.

$$$ Posada del Angel, Washington Barbot 59, T+598 (0)52-24602, www.posadadelangel.net. Expect a warm welcome at this small hotel with pool, set on a quiet street close to the historic quarter.
$$$ Posada del Gobernador, 18 de Julio 205, T+598 (0)52-23018, www.delgobernador.com. Breakfast included, charming. Recommended.
$$$ Posada Manuel de Lobo, Ituzaingó 160, T+598 (0)52-22463, www.posadamanuel delobo.com. Built in 1850. Large rooms, huge baths, parking, some smaller rooms, nice breakfast area inside and out.
$$$ Posada del Virrey, España 217, T+598 (0)52-22223, www.posadadelvirrey.com. Large rooms, some with view over bay (cheaper with small bathroom and no balcony), with breakfast. Recommended.
$$$ Radisson Colonia De Sacramento, Washington Barbot 283, T+598 (0)52- 30460, www.radissoncolonia.com. Fantastic location overlooking the quiet jetty. Stylish restaurant with fabuous views over the river.
$$$ Royal, General Flores 340, T+598 (0)52-22169, www.hotelroyalcolonia.com. Shabby lobby but pleasant rooms, some with Río de la Plata views, with breakfast, comfortable, good restaurant, pool, noisy a/c but recommended.
$$ Hostal de los Poetas, Mangarelli 675, T/F+598 (0)52-25457. With bath, quiet, pleasant. Recommended but far from the centre.
$$ Hotel Romi, Rivera 236, T+598 (0)52-30456, www.hotelromi.com.uy. Central, all rooms have private bathrooms. Parking.

Hostels
$ pp El Viajero, Washington Barbot 164, T+598 (0)52-22683, www.elviajero colonia.com. Small, friendly hostel with a/c and Wi-Fi. Some doubles (**$$**).
$ pp Hostel Colonial, General Flores 440, T+598 (0)52-30347, www.hihostels. com. Central, but noisy hostel with free bike hire and Wi-Fi. Some doubles (**$**).

$ pp **Español**, Manuel Lobo 377, T+598 (0)52-30759. Good value with shared bath in dorms, breakfast US$4, internet, kitchen. Recommended.

Camping
Camping Municipal, Real de San Carlos, T+598 (0)52-24444. US$5 per person. Mini-*cabañas* (**$$**), electric hook-ups, 100 m from beach, hot showers, open all year, safe. Recommended.

Eating

Tigre *p82*
$$$-$$ Gato Blanco, Río Capitán 80, T011-4728 0390, www.gatoblanco.com. 40-min trip by regular ferry from Tigre. Good international menu, as well as more traditional Argentine staples such as steak, pasta and pizza. Also has a bar and tea room. In elegant surroundings on terraces on the banks of the river. One of the delta's best.
$$$-$ Beixa Flor, Arroyo Abra Viejo 148, T011-4728 2397, www.beixaflor.com.ar. Lovely setting with a private beach and great music. The food is all home-made.

Colonia del Sacramento *p80, map p82*
$$$ Blanco y Negro, Gen Flores 248, T+598 (0)52-22236, www.bynresto jazz.com.uy. Closed Tue and Wed. Set in historic brick building, smart, great range of meat dishes, live jazz every night. Cellar of local wines.
$$$ Del Carmen, Washington Barbot 283. T+598 (0)52-30460. Open from breakfast to dinner, fantastic views, great for evening drink. Recommended.
$$$ Lo de Renata, Flores 227, T+598 (0)52-31061. Open daily. Popular for its lunchtime buffet of meats and salads.
$$$ Mesón de la Plaza, Vasconcellos 153, T+598 (0)52-24807. 140-year-old house with a leafy courtyard, elegant dining, good traditional food.

$$$ Viejo Barrio (VB), Vasconcellos 169, T+598 (0)52-25399. Closed Wed. Very good for home-made pastas and fish, renowned live shows.
$$$ Yacht Club (Puerto de Yates), T+598 (0)52-31354. Ideal at sunset with wonderful view of the bay. Good fish.
$$$ Arcoiris, Av Gral Flores at Plaza 25 de Agosto. Very good ice cream.
$$ Club Colonia, Gen Flores 382, T+598 (0) 52-22189. Good value, frequented by locals.
$$ El Drugstore, Portugal 174, T+598 (0)52-25241. Hip, fusion food: Latin American, European, Japanese, creative varied menu, good salads and fresh vegetables. Music and show.
$$ El Torreón, end of Av Gen Flores. T+598 (0)52-31524. One of the best places to enjoy a sunset meal with views of the river. Also a café serving toasties and cakes.
$$ La Amistad, 18 de Julio 448. Good local grill.
$$ La Bodeguita, Del Comercio 167, T+598 (0)52-25329. Tue-Sun evenings and Sat-Sun lunch. Its terrace on the river is the main attraction of this lively pizza place that also serves good *chivitos* and pasta.
$$ Lobo, Del Comercio y De la Playa, T+598 (0) 52-29245. Modern interior, good range of salads, pastas and meat. Live music at weekends.
$$ Mercosur, Flores and Ituzaingó, T+598 (0)52-24200. Popular, varied dishes. Also café serving home-made cakes.
$$ Parrillada El Portón, Gral Flores 333. T+598 (0)52-25318. Best *parillada* in town. Small, relatively smart restaurant, good atmosphere. House speciality is offal.
$$ Pulpería de los Faroles, Misiones de los Tapes 101, T+598 (0)52-30271. Very inviting tables (candlelit at night) on the cobbled streets for a varied menu that includes tasty salads, seafood and local wines.
$$-$$ El Asador, Ituzaingó 168. Good *parrillada* and pasta, nice atmosphere, value for money.

○ Shopping

Colonia del Sacramento *p80, map p82*
There's a large artist community, Uruguayan and international, with good galleries across town. There are leather shops on C Santa Rita, next to Yacht Club.
Afro, 18 de Julio 246. Candombe culture items from local black community, and percussion lessons.
Colonia Shopping, Av Roosevelt 458. Shopping mall on main road out of town (east) selling international fashion brands.
Eduardo Acosta, Paseo del Sol, Del Comercio 158. Decorative pottery by local artist.
El Almacén, Real 150. Creative gifts.
Oveja Negra, De la Playa 114. Recommended for woollen and leather clothes.

▲ Activities and tours

Tigre *p82*
Boat trips
See also Transport in Buenos Aires, page 70.
Catamarán Libertad, Puerto de Olivos. At the weekends, longer trips (4½ hrs) to the open Río de la Plata estuary.
Interisleña, Río Tigre, T011-4731 0261 and **Río Tur**, Puerto de Frutos, T011-4731 0280. Tourist catamarans, 5 services daily, 1- to 2-hr trips, US$3.50.

Colonia del Sacramento *p80, map p82*
City tours available with **Destino Viajes**, General Flores 341, T+598 (0)52-25343, destinoviajes@adinet.com.uy, or guided tours with **Sacramento Tour**, Av Flores and Rivera, T+598 (0)52 23148, sacratur@adinet.com.uy. **Asociación Guías de Colonia**, T+598 (0)52- 22309/22796, asociacionguiascolonia@gmail.com. Organizes walking tours (1 hr, US$5) in the Barrio Histórico, starting daily 1100 and 1500, from tourist office next to Old Gate.

○ Transport

San Isidro *p76*
Taxi
Turismo York, T011-4743 0561, turismo york@aol.com. Friendly and reliable taxi company, cheaper than getting a Buenos Aires company to come out to San Isidro.

Colonia del Sacramento *p80, map p82*
Book in advance for all sailings and flights in summer, especially at weekends.

Air
For airport information, see page 80. Flights to Aeroparque, **Buenos Aires**, most days, generally quicker than hydrofoil. Taxi to centre US$10.

Bus
To **Montevideo**, ½ hourly service, 2½ hrs, US$9, **COT** and **Tauril**; to **Carmelo**, Mon-Sat, 4 per day, 1½ hrs (Tauriño), US$4 Chadre/Agencia Central.
  Bus company offices **COT**, Flores 432, T+598 (0)52-23121; **Tauril**, Flores and Suárez; **Tauriño**, Flores 436.

Car hire
In bus terminal: **Avis**, T+598 (0)52-29842, US$100 per day, **Hertz**, T+598 (0)52-29851, US$90 per day. Thrifty by port, also at Flores 172, T+598 (0)52-22939, where there are bicycles too (US$3 per hr), scooters (US$7 per hr) and golf buggies (US$15 per hr) for hire, recommended as traffic is slow and easy to navigate.

Ferry
For information on ferry transport, see Buenos Aires, page 70.

Motorcycle and bicycle hire
Thrifty, Flores 172, T+598 (0)52-22939. Rent bicycles, scooters, quadbikes and golf buggies. Prices range from US$1.50 per hr

(bicycle) to US$15 per hr (golf buggy). Recommended. Traffic is slow and easy to navigate.

Directory

Colonia del Sacramento *p80, map p82*
Currency exchange **Cambio Dromer**, Flores 350 and Suárez, T+598(0)52-22070, Mon-Fri 0900-2000, Sat 0900-1800, Sun 1000-1300 (also outside the ferry dock, with car hire); **Cambio Colonia** and **Banco de la República Oriental del Uruguay** at the ferry port (dollars and South American currencies); **HSBC**, Portugal 183, Mon-Fri 1300-1700, changes money, and is located in a pretty colonial homestead.

Contents

Buenos Aires Province

The Pampas

The Pampas are home to one of the most enduring images of Argentina: the gaucho on horseback, roaming the plains. All over the Pampas there are quiet, unspoiled towns where gaucho culture is still very much alive. Two impeccably preserved gaucho towns very much worth visiting are San Antonio de Areco and Chascomús. The former is home to expert craftsmen, working silver and leather in the traditional gaucho way. Near here there are many of the finest and most historical estancias: two are recommended, El Ombú and La Bamba. Further southeast, Chascomús is similarly charming, a traditional cowboy town come to life, with pristine examples of 1870s architecture, a good museum of the Pampas and gauchos, and a lake for watersports in summer. There are fine estancias here too: friendly, relaxed La Fé, and best of all, Dos Talas, with its extraordinary history and beautiful grounds. Further inland, there are three more excellent estancias, La Concepción, Santa Rita, and the Loire chateau-style La Candelaria. Whether you stay the night or just visit for an afternoon to eat lunch and ride, you'll get an unforgettable taste of life on the land. The Pampas are also rich in wildlife, and on lakes and lagunas you're likely to spot Chilean flamingos and herons, maguari storks, white-faced ibis and black-necked swans. Ostrich-like greater rheas can also be seen in many parts. For more information, see www.turismolapampa.gov.ar (in Spanish).

Ins and outs → For listings, see pages 98-102.

Getting around It's easy to get around the province with a network of buses to and from Buenos Aires, and between towns. Train lines operate to Mar del Plata, and to Chascomús and Tandil, stopping at many coastal towns on the way. You'll need to hire a car to reach the more remote *estancias*, and there are good, fast toll roads radiating out from the capital to Mar del Plata, via Chascomús, San Antonio de Areco and Lobos. Check out www.chascomus.com.ar, www.lobos.gov.ar, www.sanantoniodeareco.com/turismo, and www.turismo.gba.gov.ar; www.turismo.gov.ar also has links to all these small towns. ▶ For further details, see Transport, page 102.

Background

Travelling through these calm lands you wouldn't think they'd had such a violent past; but these are the rich fertile plains that justified conquering the indigenous people in the bloody 19th-century Campaign of the Desert106. Once the Spanish newcomers had gained control, their produce made Argentina the 'breadbasket of the world', and the sixth richest nation on Earth, exporting beef, lamb, wheat and wool when a growing Europe demanded cheap food and clothing. When you see these huge, perfect wheat fields, and superbly healthy Aberdeen Angus cattle roaming vast plains, you might wonder how a country with such riches can possibly have suffered an economic crisis. It's one of the great enigmas of Argentina. To get an idea of Argentina's former wealth, visit an *estancia* with history, like Dos Talas, and ask their owners what went wrong. Some blame Perón, and now the Kirchners, for taxing the farmers too harshly, or Menem for resorting to desperate measures to keep up with the US dollar by selling the nationalized industries. Farmers complain the government imposes impossible taxes for those who produce from the land. The fields of Buenos Aires province provide more than half of Argentina's cereal production, and over a third of her livestock, but many *estancia* owners have had to turn to tourism in order to maintain the homes built by their ancestors in more affluent times. Still, staying in an *estancia* is a rare privilege, to be wholeheartedly enjoyed.

San Antonio de Areco → *For listings, see pages 98-102. Phone code 02326. Population 18,000.*

San Antonio de Areco, 113 km northwest of Buenos Aires, is *the* original gaucho town and makes a perfect escape from the capital. Built in the late 19th century, much of its charm lies in the authenticity of its crumbling buildings surrounding an atmospheric plaza filled with palms and plane trees, and the streets lined with orange trees. The attractive *costanera* along the riverbank is a great place to swim and picnic. There are several *estancias* nearby, and the town itself has several historical *boliches* (combined bar and provisions stores), where you can lap up the atmosphere, listen to live music and meet locals. Gaucho traditions are on display in the many weekend activities, and the town's craftsmen produce wonderful silverwork, textiles and traditional worked leather handicrafts of the highest quality. Annual events include the *pato* games in January, a poncho parade in February and the **Fiesta Criolla** in March. Most important of all, however, is the **Day of Tradition**, in the second week of November (book accommodation in advance). For more information, see Festivals and events, page 102. The **tourist information centre** ① *Parque San Martín, Zerboni and Arellano, T02326-453165,*

Gaucho life

The gaucho is the cowboy of Argentina, found all over the country, and one of Argentina's most important cultural icons. Gauchos emerged as a distinct social group in the early 18th century. Brought over by the Spanish to tend cattle, they combined their Moorish roots with Argentine Criollo stock, adopting aspects of the indigenous peoples' lifestyle, but creating their own particular style and dress. The gaucho lived on horseback, dressing in a poncho, *bombachas* (baggy trousers) held up by a *tirador* (broad leather belt) and home-made boots with leather spurs. He was armed with a *facón* or large knife, and *boleadoras*, a lasso made from three stones tied with leather thongs, which when expertly thrown would wrap around the legs of animals to bring them swiftly to the ground. Gauchos roamed the Pampas, hunting the seemingly inexhaustible herds of wild cattle and horses in the long period before fencing protected private property. The gaucho's wild reputation derived from his resistance to government officials who tried to exert their control by the use of anti-vagrancy laws and military conscription. Much of the urban population of the time regarded the gaucho as a savage, on a par with the 'indians'.

The gaucho's lifestyle was doomed in the advent of railways, fencing and the redistribution of land that followed the massacre of indigenous peoples. Increasingly the term gaucho came to mean an *estancia* worker who made a living on horseback tending cattle. As the real gaucho disappeared from the Pampas, he became a major subject of Argentine folklore and literature, most famously in José Hernández' epic poem of 1872, *Martín Fierro*, and in Güiraldes' later novel *Don Segundo Sombra*. But you can still see gauchos in their traditional dress at work today in any *estancia*. Visit Mataderos, Chascomús, or San Antonio de Areco for displays of traditional gaucho horsemanship, music, silversmithing and leatherwork.

www.sanantoniodeareco.com, has friendly, helpful, English-speaking staff who can advise on gaucho activities in the town, as well as accommodation and transport. Other useful websites include www.pagosdeareco.com.ar and www.areco.mun.gba.gov.ar.

The **Museo Gauchesco Ricardo Güiraldes** ① *Camino Güiraldes, Wed-Mon 1100-1700, US$1, guided visits Sat, Sun 1230 and 1530*, is a replica of a typical *estancia* of the late 19th century, and houses impressive gaucho artefacts and displays on the life of the writer, who was a sophisticated member of Parisian literary circles and an Argentine nationalist who romanticized gaucho life. Güiraldes spent much of his early life on **Estancia La Porteña**, 8 km from San Antonio, and settled there to write his best-known book, *Don Segundo Sombra* (1926), which was set in San Antonio. The *estancia* and sights in the town, such as the old bridge and the Pulpería La Blanqueada (at the entrance to the museum), became famous through its pages.

Superb gaucho silverwork is for sale at the workshop and **Centro Cultural y Museo Taller Draghi** ① *Lavalle 387, T02326-454219, daily 1000-1230, 1530-1900, US$1.70 for a guided visit*. You can get a further idea of the life of the gauchos at the **Mueso Las Lilas** ① *Moreno 279, T02326-456425, www.museolaslilas.org, Thu-Sun 1000-2000 (1800 in* winter) US$5, which houses a collection of paintings by famous Argentine artist Florencio Molina Campos, who dedicated his life to the display of the gaucho way of life. Excellent chocolates are made at **La Olla de Cobre** ① *Matheu 433, T02326-453105, www.laollade cobre.com.ar* , with a charming little café for drinking chocolate and trying the most amazing home-made *alfajores*. There is a large park, **Parque San Martín**, spanning the river to the north of the town near the tourist information centre. While you're here, you should visit one of the old traditional bars, or *pulperías*, many of which have been lovingly restored to recreate the 1900s ambience, and are brought to life by a genuine local clientele every night. Try **La Vieja Sodería**, on General Paz and Bolívar, or **El Almacén de Ramos Generales Parrilla**, at Zapiola 143. Also at Alsina 66 is the city museum, **Centro Cultural y Museo Usina Vieja** ① *Tue-Sun 1100-1700, US$50.* There are ATMs on the plaza, and at the country club you can play golf or watch a polo match in restful surroundings; ask at the tourist office for directions.

Some of the province's finest *estancias* are within easy reach of San Antonio for day visits, offering an *asado* lunch, horse riding and other activities. One such place is **La Cinacina** ① *T02326-452045, www.lacinacina.com.ar*, which charges US$65 per person for a day visit. For a list of those offering accommodation, see Sleeping, page 98.

La Plata → *For listings, see pages 98-102.*

The capital of Buenos Aires province is La Plata, a modern university city with a lively student population, and consequently good nightlife, with lots of restaurants and bars. There's no particular reason to visit as a tourist, but if you're passing through or on a day trip from Buenos Aires (only 60 minutes by bus), you'll appreciate the broad avenues, leafy plazas and elaborate public buildings. It's a young and vibrant place, where football and rugby are major passions. At the east of the city there's a beautiful park, **Paseo del Bosque**, popular at weekends with families for *asados*, with its famous science museum, the magnificent but slightly run-down **Museo de Ciencias Naturales**.

Ins and outs → *Phone code 0221. Population 642,000.*
Getting there La Plata is 56 km southeast of Buenos Aires, 45 minutes by car. There are frequent trains, taking one hour 10 minutes. Buses from Buenos Aires leave every 30 minutes and take about 1½ hours. They leave the Retiro bus terminal day and night, and from Plaza Constitución (less recommended), daytime only. If you arrive on an overnight bus at 0600, the *confitería* opposite the **bus terminal** (T0221-427 3186) is safe and will be open. Long-distance buses arrive here from all major cities. The terminal is at Calle 4 and Diagonal 74, and a taxi into the central area costs US$5.

Getting around The city is easy to get around, but note that the streets have numbers, rather than names, and diagonal streets cross the entire city, which can be very confusing. When you approach one of these crossroads with six choices, make sure you remember the number of the street you're on. There's an efficient network of buses all over the city, and taxis are safe, cheap and plentiful.

Tourist information The main tourist office is **Dirección de Turismo** ① *Palacio Campodónico, Diag 79 between 5 and 56, Mon-Fri 1000-1800, T0221-422 9764,*

---

www.cultura.laplata.gov.ar, www.laplata.gov.ar. There are also small **tourist booths** at Pasaje Dardo Rocha ① *on 50 between 6 and 7, T0221-427 1535, daily 1000-1700*, and in the **bus terminal** ① *on 42 between 3 and 4, Mon-Fri 0930-1330*. The provincial tourism website

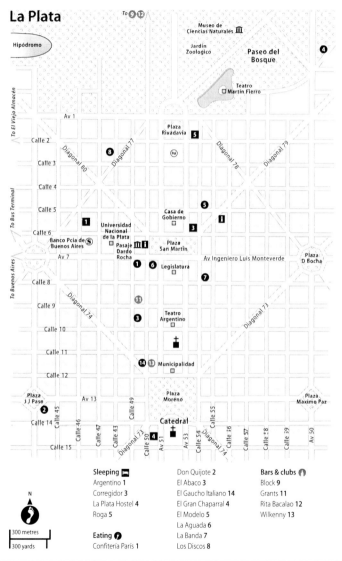

La Plata

Sleeping 🛏
Argentino **1**
Corregidor **3**
La Plata Hostel **4**
Roga **5**

Eating 🍴
Confitería París **1**

Don Quijote **2**
El Abaco **3**
El Gaucho Italiano **14**
El Gran Chaparral **4**
El Modelo **5**
La Aguada **6**
La Banda **7**
Los Discos **8**

Bars & clubs 🍸
Block **9**
Grants **11**
Rita Bacalao **12**
Wilkenny **13**

is www.turismo.gba.gov.ar (in English). A helpful office for exploring *estancias*, stables and for visiting craftsmen in the Pampas is **Camino del Gaucho** ① *57 No 393, T0221-425 7482, www.caminodelgaucho.com.ar*. The English-speaking staff are extremely informative and will help you arrange your own itinerary.

Sights

The major public buildings are centred around two parallel north-south streets, 51 and 53, which run north from the Plaza Moreno to the Plaza San Martín, and from there to the Paseo del Bosque at the north of the city centre. On the west side of Plaza Moreno is the enormous brick neo-Gothic **cathedral** ① *daily 0900-1300, 1500-1800*, built between 1885 and 1936, and inspired by Cologne and Amiens. It has a beautiful and inspiring inside, and is definitely worth a visit. Opposite is the large, white building of the **Muncipalidad**, in German Renaissance style, with a striking clock tower. Plaza San Martín, six blocks east, is bounded by the **Legislature**, with its huge neoclassical façade and, opposite, the **Casa de Gobierno** is a mixture of French and Flemish Renaissance styles. On the north side of the plaza is the lovely **Pasaje Dardo Rocha**, designed as the main railway station in Italian Renaissance style. It now houses the **Centro Cultural** ① *Calle No 50 between 6 and 7, T0221-427 1843, gallery Mon-Fri 1000-1300, 1500-1800, Sat and Sun 1500-1800, free*, with a gallery of contemporary Latin American art, a café and two theatres. East of the Municipalidad, **Teatro Argentino** has its own orchestra and ballet company. Nearby on streets 6 and 7 are the imposing **Universidad Nacional** and the **Banco Provincial**. The main shopping streets are 8 and 12. A good market selling handicrafts and local *artesania* is in Plaza Italia at weekends.

If you do find yourself in La Plata at the weekend, or on a sunny evening, head straight for **Paseo del Bosque**, a pretty public park of woodlands and an artificial lake, where all the locals head for *asados* and picnics. There's also the **Zoological Gardens** with giraffes, elephants and pumas amongst others, an astronomical observatory and the Hipodromo, dating from the 1930s and one of the most important racecourses in the country. The **Museo de Ciencias Naturales** ① *T011-425 7744, www.fcnym.unlp.edu.ar/ museo, daily 1000- 1800, US$2, free guided tours, Mon-Fri 1400 and 1600, Sat-Sun hourly, in Spanish and in English (phone first to request)*, is one of the most famous museums in Latin America. It houses an outstanding collection, particularly on anthropology and archaeology, with a huge collection of pre-Columbian artefacts including pre-Incan ceramics from Peru, and beautiful ceramics from the northwest of Argentina. It is slightly run-down with some exhibits needing replacing but the preserved animal and dinosaur sections are worth visiting.

Around La Plata → For listings, see pages 98-102.

Eight kilometres northwest of the city, the **República de los Niños** ① *Col General Belgrano and Calle 501, T011-484 1409, www.republica.laplata.gov.ar, daily 1000-2200, US$1, children free, parking US$1.30*, is Eva Perón's legacy, built under the first Perón administration, a delightful children's village, with scaled-down castles, oriental palaces, boating lake, cafés and even a little train. It's a fun place for families to picnic.

This area of the country has some lovely rural accommodation. A delightful option close to La Plata is the **Casa de Campo La China** ① *T0221-421 2931, www.casadecampola china.com.ar*, a charming 1930s adobe house set in eucalyptus woods, with beautifully

Argentine steak

So how did Argentina come to be synonymous with great beef? Cattle certainly aren't indigenous to the Pampas. But after Juan de Garay's expedition in 1580 brought cattle from Paraguay, the animals roamed wild on the fertile plains, reproducing so quickly that by the time the Spanish returned in 1780, there were 40 million of them. But by then, local indigenous groups were making a roaring trade, driving herds of cattle through the Andean passes to sell in southern Chile. Gauchos, meanwhile, were hunting cattle with the use of *boleadoras* (a lasso with three stone balls), and slaughtering them by the thousand for their hides alone, sometimes leaving the meat to rot. When salting plants – *saladeros* – arrived in 1810, the hides were transported to Europe, together with tallow for candles. The meat was turned into *charqui*, cut into strips, dried and salted, and sold to feed slaves in Brazil and Cuba. It was only with the invention of refrigerated ships that Argentina's produce was exported to meet the growing demand for beef in an expanding Europe. Cattle farmers introduced new breeds to replace the scrawny Pampas cattle, and sowed alfalfa as richer fodder than pampas grasses. Today Herefords and Aberdeen Angus are still bred for meat.

And why is Argentine beef so good? Because these cows are healthy! With such vast expanses of land to roam, the cattle burn off any fat, are well-toned and lean: the meat is even high in Omega 3. So head straight for the best *parrilla* in town, and, unless you're vegetarian, try a few different cuts. Better still, stay at an *estancia* to try home-reared beef cooked on the *asado*, the traditional way over an open wood fire. Delicious. A word of warning: learn some of the names for the parts of a cow so you don't end up eating hoof, intestines or glands. See the menu reader, page 118.

furnished accommodation and far-reaching views. Stay with the charming English-speaking family, or visit for the day, ride horses and enjoy carriage rides.

Parque Costero Sur Reserve and Estancia Juan Gerónimo

Parque Costero Sur is a large nature reserve 110 km south of La Plata, and 160 km south of Buenos Aires – just two hours' drive away. Declared a UNESCO Biosphere Site in 1997, it extends along 70 km of the coastline of Bahía Samborombón, and was created to protect a wide range of birds that come here to breed. There are several *estancias* inside the reserve including the beautiful 1920s Tudor-style **Estancia Juan Gerónimo** ① *T0221-481 414, www.juangeronimo.com.ar.* The 4000-ha *estancia* is magnificently situated right on the coast, and from here you can enjoy walking or horse riding in total peace and quiet – you can ride for three days here without ever repeating a route. The *estancia* is more of a village than a house, with a collection of Tudor-style buildings in the lovely grounds, including a tea house, a little cabin, stables and a rural school. The main house has a wonderful old library with an extensive collection of books on pre-Columbian culture, as well as literature in French, English and German. Its 11 guest bedrooms are beautifully decorated but best of all is the warm welcome you'll receive from the relaxed owner, Florencia Molinuevo. As well as horse riding along the coast, dunes and pampas, there's superb birdwatching and opportunities for swimming.

Chascomús → *For listings, see pages 98-102.*

This quaint historical town, 126 km south of Buenos Aires, is worth visiting to enjoy the vibrant combination of gaucho culture and fine 19th-century architecture, creating an atmosphere of colonial refinement with a Wild West feel. Chascomús was founded in 1779, when a fort was built as protection against the indigenous tribes. In 1839, it was the site of the Battle of the Libres del Sur (the Free of the South), and its streets are full of well-preserved buildings dating from the mid-1800s, and lined with mature trees. Despite the strong historical significance, the town has a lively feel and its position along the eastern edge of the huge Laguna Chascomús gives it an attractive *costanera*, which comes to life in summer. The **tourist office** ① *Av Costanera España y Espigón de Pesca, T02241-430405, www.chascomus.com.ar, and www.chascomus.net, daily 0900-1900*, is four blocks from the main avenue, Las Astras. You can take a boat out on the *laguna*, or head to a couple of fine *estancias* nearby.

Sights → *Phone code 02241. Population 40,000.*

Around the quiet Plaza Independencia are the fudge-coloured colonial-style **Palacio Municipal** and **Iglesia Catedral**. Southeast of the plaza is the extraordinary **Capilla de los Negros** (1862) ① *daily 1000-1200, 1700-1900*, a small brick chapel with earth floor, built as a place of worship for African slaves who were bought by wealthy families in the early 1800s; it's an atmospheric place that still holds the slaves' offerings. A highly recommended museum for an insight into gaucho culture is the **Museo Pampeano** ① *Av Lastra and Muñiz, T02241-425110, www.chascomus.com.ar/museo_pampeano2.php, daily 0900-1500, US$0.50*, which has lots of information on gaucho traditions, fabulous maps of the Spanish conquest, furniture and all the evident wealth of the early pioneers.

To the south of the town lies the **Laguna Chascomús**, one of a chain of seven connected lakes; the *costanera* is a pleasant place to stroll, you can sail and windsurf in the summer, and there are frequent regattas. It's also an important breeding site for *pejerrey* fish, with amateur fishing competitions held from November to March. The delightful *estancia* **La Fe** ① *www.estancialafe.com*, is nearby.

Dolores → *For listings, see pages 98-102. Phone code 02245. Population 30,000.*

Dolores is a pretty, sleepy little town, 204 km south of Buenos Aires. Founded in 1818, it was the first town in independent Argentina, and its attractive old buildings would be perfect as a film set for a 19th-century drama. There's an interesting little museum, **Museo Libres del Sur** ① *Parque Libres del Sur, daily 1000-1700*, with good displays on local history, in particular about the Campaign of the Desert and the subsequent revolt against Rosas. It also contains lots of gaucho silver, plaited leather *tableros*, branding irons and a huge cart from 1868. There's a charming plaza at the heart of the town, with a central obelisk and impressive classical-style church, the **Iglesia Nuestra Señora de Dolores**. In mid- to late February, the **Fiesta de la Guitarra** is held, with performances from internationally famous musicians, dancing and processions. This is a good time to visit, but book ahead. For further information, contact the **tourist office** ① *T02245-442432, www.dolores.gov.ar*. The railway station is 15 minutes' walk from the centre.

Estancia Dos Talas

The main reason to visit Dolores is its proximity to one of the oldest and most beautiful *estancias* in the Pampas, **Dos Talas** ① *10 km south of Dolores, 2 hrs' drive from Buenos Aires, T02245-443020, www.dostalas.com.ar*. The fabulously elegant house is set in grand parkland designed by Charles Thays, with a lovely chapel copied from Notre Dame de Passy and a fascinating history. Come for the day or, even better, stay. You'll be warmly welcomed by the owners, who are descendants of the *estancia*'s original owner, Pedro Luro. This beautifully decorated home is one of Argentina's really special places to stay.

The Pampas listings

For Sleeping and Eating price codes and other relevant information, see pages 11-17.

⊞ Sleeping

San Antonio de Areco *p91*

$$$ Antigua Casona, Segunda Sombra 495, T02326-456600, www.antiguacasona.com. Charmingly restored 1897 house with 5 rooms opening onto a delightful patio and exuberant garden, very relaxing.

$$$ Paradores Draghi, Lavalle 385, T02326-455 583, www.paradoresdraghi.com.ar. Beautifully renovated old colonial building, with traditional-style rooms, very comfortable, with kitchen and bathroom. Recommended.

$$$ Patio de Moreno, Moreno 251, T02326-455197, www.patiodemoreno.com. Stunning modern rooms, in the middle of town, set in a wonderfully old building. Small pool, personal service and a cosy living room.

$$ Hostal de Areco, Zapiola 25, T02326-456 118, www.hostaldeareco.com.ar. Popular, with a warm welcome, very good value.

$$ Los Abuelos, Zerboni and Zapiola, T02326-456390. Neat hotel with well-equipped rooms and a small pool. Simple, modern-ish but comfortable.

$$ San Carlos, Zerboni and Zapiola, T02326-453106, www.hotel-sancarlos.com.ar. Simple and friendly hotel near the river with a small pool and only a short walk to the main plaza.

$$ Posada del Ceibo, Irigoyen and Smith, T02326-454614, www.laposadadel ceibo.com.ar. Old-fashioned family place that looks like a bit like a 1950s motel. Basic rooms and a pool in the garden.

Estancias

Some of the province's finest *estancias* are within easy reach of San Antonio for day visits but it's best to stay overnight to appreciate the peace and beauty of these historical places. The following are recommended:

$$$$ El Ombú, T02326-492080 (T011-4710 2795, office in Buenos Aires), Mon-Fri, www.estanciaelombu.com. A fine Italian neoclassical house with magnificent terrace, dating from 1890, with comfortable old-fashioned bedrooms, furnished with antiques. Offers horse riding and a warm welcome from English-speaking owners, the Boelcke family. The price includes meals, drinks and activities, but not transfer. *Día de Campo* (day on the ranch), US$70 per person. Taxi from Ezeiza US$115, from Buenos Aires centre or internal airport Aeroparque, US$90.

$$$$ El Rosario de Areco, T02326-451000, www.rosariodeareco.com.ar. A 19th-century house in lovely parkland, this is a traditional *estancia* for breeding polo ponies, and the children of the owners are keen polo players. Not surprisingly, there's excellent horse riding here, as well as a high standard of accommodation in attractive rooms, and superb food. Also 2 swimming pools.

$$$$ Estancia La Porteña, Ruta 8, Km 110, T011-155626 7347, www.laporteniadeareco. com. One of Argentina's most famous *estancias* which was once host to writers

Ricardo Güiraldes and Antoine de Saint Exupéry. Stunning traditional building built in 1822, original features, large grounds with 150-year-old trees and working horses. There are 3 lovely houses where you can stay, including huge banquets of food (lots of meat), or you can spend a day here, enjoying the grounds.

$$$$ La Bamba, T02326-456293 (T011-47321 269, office in Buenos Aires), www.la-bamba.com.ar. A plum-coloured, colonial-style building dating from 1830 with a fascinating history. It was originally a post-house on the Camino Royal (royal road) connecting Buenos Aires with the north of the country. It was the first *estancia* to open to guests in the 1930s, and has attracted many famous visitors since then. It's set in beautiful parkland, with charming rooms and welcoming English-speaking owners, the Aldao family, who have lived here for generations. It's very relaxing, with only 5 rooms and highly recommended. Serves superb meals.

$$$ Santa Rita, near Lobos, 120 km west of Buenos Aires, T02227-495026, www.santa-rita.com.ar. Spectacular building in gorgeous lakeside setting where the Nüdemberg family make you welcome in their eccentric, late 18th-century home. Great fun, US$47 per person for a day visit. Highly recommended.

Camping
Auto-camping La Porteña, 12 km from town on the **Güiraldes Estancia**, good earth access roads. A beautiful spot with many *parrilladas* at picnic spots along the bank of the Río Areco.
Club River Plate, Av del Valle and Alvear, T02326-452744. The best of 3 sites in the park by the river. It's an attractive sports club offering shady sites with all facilities, a pool and sports of all kinds, US$6 per tent.

La Plata *p93, map p94*
Most hotels here are business-orientated.

$$$ Hotel Argentino, Calle 46, No 536, between 5 and 6, T0221-423 4111, www.hotelargentino. com. Comfortable and very central, with bright rooms, all with bath and floral sheets. Also has apartments to rent.
$$$ Hotel Corregidor, Calle 6, No1026, between 53 and 54, T0221-425 6800, www.hotelcorregidor.com.ar. An upmarket, modern business hotel, with well-furnished rooms with bath, pleasant public rooms. Good value.
$$ Hotel Roga, Calle 54, No334, between 1 and 2, T0221-421 9553, www.hotelroga. com.ar. Basic, clean rooms, on a quiet street a short walk from the main plazas.

Hostels
$ pp **La Plata Hostel**, Calle 50 No1066, T0221-457 1424, www.laplata-hostel.com.ar. Only 2 blocks from the cathedral, this hostel is well organized and set in a lovely turn-of-the-century house. High ceilings, original doors and a small garden to relax in. Simple but comfortable dorms.

Around La Plata *p95*
Estancias
$$$$ Estancia Juan Gerónimo, T0221-481414, www.juangeronimo.com.ar. 170 km south of Buenos Aires, 2 hrs' drive. The perfect place to relax in really elegant accommodation, this is a beautiful Tudor-style house right on the shore of the Río de la Plata, set in its own nature reserve, with 3238 ha of beach, dunes, forest and pampas to explore. You'll be personally welcomed by the charming owner Florencia and her family, who will take you riding or birdwatching, and share with you the *estancia*'s interesting history. Wonderful riding and food. Full board, all meals and activities included. English and French spoken. Day visit US$65. See also page 96.
$$$ Casa de Campo La China, 60 km from La Plata on R11, T0221-421 2931, www.casadecampolachina.com.ar. Beautifully

decorated, spacious rooms off an open gallery, with great views. Day rates available. Charming hosts speak perfect English. Delicious food. Highly recommended.

Chascomús *p97*

There are a few very reasonably priced places to stay in town with more upmarket accommodation to be found in the apart hotels and *cabañas* near the lake shore. See www.chascomus.com.ar for a complete list.

$$$ Mi EspacioSur, Ayacucho 640, T02241-431786, www.miespaciosur.com.ar. Modern hotel, with clean doubles and triples. Large pool, and each room leads out onto a deck. Much cheaper during the week (**$$**).

$$$ Noble Blanco, Mazzini 130, T02241- 436 3235, www.robleblanco.com.ar. By far the best place to stay in town. Modern comfortable rooms, a large heated pool with attractive deck and welcoming common areas, all in a refurbished 100-year-old house. Also a spa offering massages, sauna and treatments. Recommended.

$$ Chascomus, Lastra 367, T02241-422968, www.chascomus.com.ar. Stylish, turn-of-the-century public rooms and lovely terrace, this is an atmospheric and welcoming place. Breakfast is included and the staff are friendly.

$$ El Mirador, Belgrano 485, T02241-422273. An attractively renovated old building, with simple rooms but lovely original details in the public rooms. Spotlessly clean and simple.

Estancias

$$$$ Estancia La Fe, R2, Km 116, T02241-155 42095, www.estancialafe.com.ar. A charming and typical place to come for a few days to get a feel for life on the land. Activities include horse riding, riding in carriages and walking in the grounds. Simple, comfortable rooms, wide views from the grounds, great *asado*.

$$$$ Haras La Viviana, 45 km from Chascomús, T011-4702 9633, www.laviviana com.ar. Perfect for horse riding as fine polo ponies are bred here. Tiny cabins in gardens by a huge *laguna* where you can kayak or fish. Very peaceful, wonderful welcome from the lady novelist owner who speaks fluent English. Can arrange collection from Chascomús.

$$$ La Horqueta, 3 km from Chascomús on R20, T011-4777 0150, www.lahorqueta.com. An 1898 Tudor-style mansion, lovely grounds with a *laguna* for fishing, horse riding, bikes to borrow. It's a good place for children, with safe gardens to explore. 9 comfortable, lovely rooms, food is nothing special.

Camping

There are 7 sites all with good facilities: **Monte Corti** is closest, 2.2 km away, T0221-430767, but there are 5 on the far side of the *laguna*, including **La Alameda**, 12.6 km away, T0221-1568 4076; **Mutual 6 de Septiembre**, 8 km away, T011-155 182 3836, has a pool.

Dolores *p97*

$$$$ Estancia Dos Talas, 10 km from Dolores, T02245-443020, www.dostalas.com.ar. One of the oldest *estancias*, you are truly the owners' guests here. The rooms and the service are impeccable, the food exquisite; stay for days, and completely relax. Pool, riding, English spoken. See also page 98.

$$ Hotel Plaza, Castelli 75, T02245-442362. Comfortable and welcoming old place on the plaza, all rooms with bath and TV, breakfast extra, good *confitería* downstairs. There's another good café next door.

Camping

Camping del Náutico, Lago Parque Náutico.

🍴 Eating

San Antonio de Areco *p91*
$$ Almacén de Ramos Generales, Zapiola
143, T02326-456376, www.ramosgenerales
areco.com.ar. Historical and very atmospheric
old bar, or *pulpería*, dating from 1850; the
perfect place to have a superb *asado*, or try
regional dishes such as *locro*.
$$ El Almacén, Bolívar 66. Popular with
locals, serving good food in an original 1900s
store.
$$ La Costa, Zerboni and Belgrano, on the
costanera near the park. Delicious *parrilla*.
$$ La Filomena, Vieytes 395. An elegant,
modern restaurant serving delicious food,
with live music at weekends. Recommended.
$ La Vuelta de Gato, opposite the park.
Good pizzas, local salami and *patero* wine.

La Plata *p93, map p94*
$$ El Gaucho Italiano, Diagonal 74 corner
of Calle 50, T0221-421 5500. Large restaurant
with friendly staff and a great menu of pizzas,
pastas and sandwiches. They have another
nicer restaurant on Calle 50, No 724 between
Calles 9 and 10, T0221-483 2817.
$$ El Modelo, Calle 54 and 5. A traditional
cervecería, with a good range on its menu,
and great beer in German-style surroundings.
$$ Los Discos, Calle 48, No 441, T0221-424
9160. The best *parrilla* in town, superb steaks.
$ Don Quijote, Plaza Paso 146. A very good
restaurant, delicious food in welcoming
surroundings. Well known and loved.
$ El Gran Chaparral, Calles 60 and 117
(Paseo del Bosque). More basic *parrillada*
situated in the lovely park.
$ La Aguada, Calle 50, between Calles 7 and
8. The oldest restaurant in town is more for
minutas (light meals) than big dinners, but
famous for its *papas fritas* (chips); the chip
soufflé is amazing.
2 fashionable places serving superb food:
El Abaco, Calle 49 between 9 and 10, and **La
Banda**, Calle 8 and 54, T0221-425 9521.

Cafés
Confitería París, corner of Calle 7 and Calle
49. The best croissants, and a great place for
coffee.

Chascomús *p97*
$$ El Viejo Lobo, Mitre and Dolores. Good
fish.
$ El Colonial, Lastra and Belgrano. Great
food, and very cheap, traditional old *parrilla*.

Dolores *p97*
$$ Restaurant La Farola, Buenos Aires 140.
Welcoming, serves good pasta dishes.
$ Parrilla Don Pedro, Av del Valle and
Crámer. Ignore the unimaginitive decor,
order steak.
$ Pizzería Cristal, Buenos Aires 226. Pizzas.

🍸 Bars and clubs

San Antonio de Areco *p91*
Pulpería La Ganas, Vieytes and Pellegrini.
An authentic, traditional old bar, full of
ancient bottles. Live music at weekends, from
2200.

La Plata *p93, map p94*
The following bars are popular and lively:
Block, corner of Calles 122 and 50, and **Rita
Bacalao**, in Gonnet, a pleasant residential
area to the north of the city.
The Grants, Calle 49 corner of 9. Lively bar
with cheap *tenedor libre* food.
Wilkenny, Calle 50 corner of 11. Hugely
popular, Irish-style pub.

🎭 Entertainment

La Plata *p93, map p94*
El Viejo Almacén, Diagonal 74 and 2. Tango
and tropical music.
Teatro Martín Fierro, Paseo del Bosque.
Free concerts during the summer.

⊛ Festivals and events

San Antonio de Areco *p91*
Nov Day of Tradition, www.visiteareco. com/es/tradicion.php. Traditional parades, gaucho games, events on horseback, music and dance.

⚠ Activities and tours

San Antonio de Areco *p91*
Country Club, R8, Km 11, T02326-453073. Play golf (US$9) or watch a polo match in restful surroundings. Good food is also served. Ask tourist office for directions.

⊖ Transport

San Antonio de Areco *p91*
Bus
To **Buenos Aires**, every hr, 2 hrs, US$7, Chevallier or Pullman General Belgrano.

La Plata *p93, map p94*
Bus
To **Buenos Aires**, every 30 mins, 1½ hrs, US$3.

Train
To **Buenos Aires** (Constitución), run by TMR, frequent, 1 hr 10 mins, US$1. The ticket office is at Constitución, hidden behind shops opposite platform 6.

Chascomús *p97*
Bus
Frequent services, several per day, to **Buenos Aires**, US$9; **La Plata**; **Mar del Plata**; and daily to **Bahía Blanca**; **Tandil**; and **Villa Gesell**, with El Cóndor and El Rápido. To **Río de la Plata** with La Estrella.

Train
To **Buenos Aires** (Constitución), 2 daily, US$5, 1st class. Also 1 a week to **Tandil** and daily to **Mar del Plata**.

Dolores *p97*
Bus
To **Buenos Aires**, 3 hrs, US$14, and to **La Plata**, US$8, El Rápido T02245-441109.

Taxi
There is a stand at Belgrano and Rico, 1 block from plaza, T02245-443507.

Train
Daily service to **Buenos Aires**, US$7 .

Southern Sierras

The south of Buenos Aires province has two ranges of ancient mountains rising suddenly from the flat Pampas; both are easily accessible and offer great opportunities for a weekend escape. The Sierra de Tandil range, due south from Buenos Aires, is 340 km long and 2000 million years old – among the oldest in the world. The beautiful, curved hills of granite and basalt offer wonderful walking and riding, with the pleasant airy town of Tandil as a base. There are plenty of small hotels, though nearby estancias offer the best way to explore the hills.

Further west, the magnificent Sierra de la Ventana is the highest range of hills in the Pampas, and so called because craggy Cerro de la Ventana has a natural hole near its summit. Next to the Parque Provincial Ernesto Tornquist, it is within easy reach of Bahía Blanca for a day or weekend visit, and the attractive villages of Villa Ventana and Sierra de la Ventana nearby are appealing places to stay, with plenty of accommodation options. These mountains are not quite as old as those in Tandil, but offer more demanding hikes in wilder terrain, with stunning views from their summits. There are daily buses and combis from Bahía Blanca, but you could break the journey at the quaint sleepy town of Tornquist.

Tornquist → *For listings, see pages 107-110. Phone code 0291. Population 6066.*

Tornquist, 70 km north of Bahía Blanca, is a pretty, sleepy, rural town that you will pass through if travelling to Sierra de la Ventana via Route 33. It has an attractive church on the large central plaza (which is more like a tidy park), a strangely green artificial lake, and a big children's play area. It's not a touristy place, but that's precisely its appeal, and it's a good starting point for excursions into the sierras. About 11 km east of town is the Tornquist family mansion (not open to tourism), built in a mixture of French styles. The town is named after Ernesto Tornquist (1842-1908) the son of a Buenos Aires merchant of Swedish origin. Under his leadership the family established an important industrial investment bank and Tornquist helped to establish the country's first sugar refinery, meat-packing plant and several chemical plants. There's a **tourist office** ⓘ *Plaza Ernesto Tornquist, 9 de Julio and Alem, T0291-494 0081, www.tornquist.gov.ar*, for information.

Parque Provincial Ernesto Tornquist → *For listings, see pages 107-110. Phone code 0291.*

The sierras are accessed from the Parque Provincial Ernesto Tornquist which is 25 km east of Tornquist on Route 76. There are two main access points, one at the foot of Cerro Ventana and the other one, further east, at the foot of Cerro Bahía Blanca. It's US$2 to enter the park. Other than the Campamento Base (see below), the nearest places for accommodation are the two towns of Sierra de la Ventana and Villa Ventana. ►► For transport to the park, see page 110.

Cerro Ventana
ⓘ *To enter this section of the park, turn left after the massive ornate gates from the Tornquist family home. There are showers and a food kiosk.*
There is an **information point** ⓘ *Dec-Easter daily 0800-1700*, and *guardaparques* who you can ask for advice and register with for the longer walks. Nearby is the hospitable **Campamento Base** ⓘ *T0291-156 495 304, www.haciafuera.com.ar/campamentobase.htm*, with hot showers, dormitory accommodation and an attractive campsite. From this entrance, it's a three-hour walk, clearly marked, but with no shade, up **Cerro de la Ventana** (1136 m), which has fantastic views from the 'window' in the summit ridge. Register with *guardaparques* and set off no later than midday. Alternative hikes are a gentle stroll to **Garganta Olvidada** (one hour each way), where you can set off up to 1700, to the **Piletones**, small pools (two hours each way), and **Garganta del Diablo** (six hours return) a wonderful narrow gorge with waterfalls. Guides are available for the walk to Garganta Olvidada, for a minimum of 10 people.

Cerro Bahía Blanca
The entrance to this section of the park is 4 km further east along Route 76. There's a car park and **interpretation centre** ⓘ *T0291-491 0039, Dec-Easter 0800-1800*, with *guardaparques* who can advise on walks. From here you can go on a guided visit to **Cueva del Toro** (only with your own vehicle, four to five hours), natural caves, and the **Cueva de las Pinturas Rupestres** which contains petroglyphs. There are also good walks, including up **Cerro Bahía Blanca** (two hours return), a gentle climb rewarded with panoramic views, highly recommended. There's lots of wildlife to spot, but you're most likely to see grey foxes, guanacos, wild horses and red deer.

Villa Ventana

Some 10 km further from the park's second entrance (Cerro Bahía Blanca section) is an attractive laid-back wooded settlement with weekend homes, *cabañas* for rent and a municipal campsite by the river with all facilities. There's an excellent tea shop, **Casa de Heidi**, and good food served in rustic surroundings at **Las Golondrinas**. The pretty village is the base for climbing **Cerro Tres Picos** (1239 m), to the south of the park, which is the highest peak in the province. The ruins of the **Hotel Club Casino** (1911) can still be seen; once the most luxurious hotel in Argentina, it burned down in 1983. There's a helpful **tourist office** ① *T0291-491 0001*, at the entrance to the village.

Sierra de la Ventana → *Phone code 0291. Population 1800.*

Continuing east, the town of Sierra de la Ventana is a good base for exploring the hills, with a greater choice of hotels than Villa Ventana, and wonderful open landscapes all around. There is an 18-hole golf course and good trout fishing in the Río Sauce Grande. There's also a wonderful tea shop, **La Angelita**, in the leafy lanes of Villa Arcadia (across the river), and several places on the river to bathe. The helpful **tourist information** ① *Av Roca 15, just before railway track, T0291-491 5303, www.sierradelaventana.org.ar*, has a complete list of all hotels, *cabañas* and campsites with availability and prices.

Tandil → *For listings, see pages 107-110. Phone code 02293. Population 101,000.*

Tandil is an attractive town, with a light breezy feel, and a centre for outdoor activities, making it a good base for exploring the nearby sierras. There are a couple of marvellous *estancias* in the area and a clutch of restaurants, cafés and bars within the town. On the south side of the main Plaza Independencia are the neoclassical **Municipalidad** (1923), the former **Banco Hipotecario Nacional** (1924) and the **Iglesia del Santísimo Sacramento** (1878), inspired (apparently) by the Sacre Coeur in Paris. Six blocks south of the plaza, up on a hill, is the **Parque Independencia**, with a granite entrance in Italianate style, built by the local Italian community to celebrate the town's centenary. Inside the park, the road winds up to a vantage point, where there's a Moorish-style **castle**, built by the Spanish community to mark the same event, with marvellous views over the surrounding sierras. At the base of the hill is an amphitheatre, where a famous community theatre event takes place during Easter week (book accommodation ahead). South of the park is the **Lago del Fuerte**, a popular place for water sports; bathing is possible at the Balneario del Sol in a complex of several swimming pools. For more information on the city, see www.tandil.com (in Spanish).

West of the plaza on the outskirts of town is **Cerro Calvario**, an easy walk leading to the **Capilla Santa Gemma** at the top. Further away, 5 km from town, **Cerro El Centinela** has a large, attractive, family-oriented tourist complex that includes a 1200-m cable car ride, a good restaurant (book your table in advaance) and swimming pools.

It's easy to get out of the city to explore the hilly countryside on foot or by bike. Heading south past the lake, follow Avenida Don Bosco or one of the nearby tree-lined roads into the beautiful surroundings. Note that you should not enter any private land without permission. Instead, contact local tour operators who have arranged exclusive access with the land owners. The main **tourist information office** ① *at the access to town (next to R226), Av Cte Espora 1120, T02293-432 225, Mon-Sat 0800-2000, Sun 0900-1300,*

The Conquest of the Desert

Until the 1870s, the Pampas, and indeed most of Argentina, was inhabited by indigenous tribes. After independence, President Rosas launched the first attempt to claim territory in Buenos Aires province in his 1833 Campaign of the Desert. But in the 1870s, pressure grew for a campaign to defeat the indigenous people, since the withdrawal of Argentine troops to fight in the War of Triple Alliance had led to a series of increasingly audacious raids by *malones*, the indigenous armies. War minister Alsina planned a series of forts and ramparts to contain the indigenous peoples, and defend the territory won from them. But his successor General Julio Roca found these plans too defensive, and called for a war of extermination, aiming to make the whole of Patagonia available for settlement. Roca's Conquest of the Desert was launched in 1879, with 8000 troops in five divisions, one of them led by Roca himself. Five important indigenous chiefs were captured, along with 1300 warriors. A further 2300 were killed or wounded. Roca's view was that 'it is a law of human nature that the Indian succumb to the impact of civilized man'. He destroyed villages and forced the inhabitants to choose between exile in Chile, or life in a reservation. After the campaign, mountain passes to Chile were closed, and any remaining indigenous groups were cruelly forced onto reservations.

Although Roca claimed victory in the Conquest of the Desert as a personal triumph, he was aided by technological advances: the telegraph gave commanders intelligence reports to offset the indigenous peoples' knowledge of the terrain and enabled them to co-ordinate their efforts. Railways moved troops swiftly, and Remington repeating rifles enabled any one soldier to take on five indigenous people and murder them all.

Roca was hailed as a hero, elected president in 1880, and dominated Argentine politics until his death in 1904. The land he conquered was handed out mainly to Roca's friends, since the campaign had been funded by mortgaging plots in advance, with bonds worth 25,000 acres being bought by only 500 people. Argentina has yet to come to terms with this shameful part of its history. But you can see that most statues of Roca throughout the country have been defaced with red paint symbolizing the blood he spilt. There is no attempt made by the authorities to stop this. In Buenos Aires the statue of Roca is on the corner of Perú and Roca, and it is covered in graffiti which is neither removed nor cleaned, unlike other public monuments.

---

is very well organized and has good brochures and urban maps. There are other offices in the **main plaza** ① *near the corner of General Rodríguez NS Pinto, Mon-Fri 0600-1300, 1800-2000, www.tandil.gov.ar*, and at the **bus terminal** ① *Av Buzón 650, T02293-432092, Mon-Sat 0800-1800, Sun 0700-1900*, 12 blocks northeast of the centre. The **railway station** ① *Av Machado and Colón, T02293- 423002*, is 15 blocks north of the plaza.

Six kilometres south is the 140-ha **Reserva Natural Sierra del Tigre**, with good views over Tandil from **Cerro Venado**. Wild foxes and guanacos can be seen occasionally, as well as llamas.

Southern Sierras listings

For Sleeping and Eating price codes and other relevant information, see pages 11-17.

😴 Sleeping

Tornquist *p104*

$$ San José, Güemes 138, T0291-494 0152, www.sanjose-hotel.com.ar. A small, central hotel with faded, simple rooms.

Villa Ventana *p105*

See www.villaventana.com for a complete list.
$$ El Mirador, R76, Km 226, before reaching Villa Ventana, T0291-494 1338, www.complejoelmirador.com.ar. Great location at the foot of Cerro Ventana with basic rooms and a good restaurant.
$$ San Hipólito, R76, Km 230, T0291-156 428 281. A few fully furnished, small, comfortable houses in a large ranch with welcoming owners, Polito and his wife. Ideal for families with kids. Enjoyable horse rides in the hills.

Sierra de la Ventana *p105*

See www.sierradelaventana.org.ar.
$$ Alihuen, Calle M Frontini and E Torquist, T0291-491 5074, www.com-tur.com.ar/alihuen. A delightful old place near the river.
$$ Cabañas La Caledonia, Los Robles and Ombúes, on leafy Villa Arcadia, T0291-491 5268, www.lacaledonia.com.ar. Well-equipped and comfortable *cabañas* in large gardens.
$$ Las Vertientes, R76, Km 221, T0291-491 0064, www.com-tur.com.ar/lasvertientes. A long-established ranch with charming hosts and an attractive main house. A beautiful location for outdoor activities or just for relaxing in peaceful surroundings.
$$ Provincial, Drago 130, T0291-491 5024, hotelprovincial@laredsur.com.ar. An old 1940s state-owned hotel, more quaint than comfy, but with good views, restaurant and a pool. Very good value.

Tandil *p105*

See www.tandil.com for a complete list.
$$$$ Ave María, Paraje la Portena, T02993-422843, www.avemariatandil.com.ar. One of the most exquisite small hotels in the whole province, this may call itself a *hostería*, but the splendid Norman-style building set in beautiful gardens overlooking the rocky summits of the sierras is much more like an *estancia*. Charming owner Asunti encourages you to feel completely at home and ramble around the place as you please. There are only 8 rooms, all impeccably designed with everything you could possibly need, some with doors opening directly onto the gardens. The discreet staff speak perfect English. A great place to relax and swim in the pool or walk in the grounds, hills and woodland. Prices are half-board and discounts apply Mon-Thu. Highly recommended, not to be missed.
$$$ Cabañas Brisas Serranas, Scavini y Los Corales, T02293-406110, www.brisas serranas.com.ar. Very comfortable and well-furnished *cabañas*, pool, lovely views and welcoming owners.
$$$ El Solar de las Magnolias, Ituzaingo 941, T02293-428618, www.solarmagnolias.com.ar. New apartment complex of lovely roomy traditional single-storey buildings, with a mix of antique and modern furniture. Parking and breakfast included.
$$$ Las Acacias, Av Brasil 642, T02293-423373, www.posadalasacacias.com.ar. *Hostería* in a restored 1890s dairy farm in the Golf Club area, with very comfortable rooms looking out on to large gardens with a splendid pool. Friendly owners who speak English and Italian, and excellent staff help to create a welcoming and homely atmosphere for a delightful stay. Recommended.
$$ Chacra Bliss, Paraje La Porteña, T02293-1562 0202, www.cybertandil.com.ar/chacrabliss. Charmingly decorated rooms

Estancias

Argentina's *estancias* vary enormously from ostentatious mansions to simple colonial-style ranches that still work as cattle farms. Many now open their doors to tourists as paying guests, enabling you to experience traditional Argentine rural life. There are two main types of *estancia*: those that function as rural hotels, and those where you're welcomed as a guest of the family. The latter are particularly recommended as a great way to meet Argentine people. You dine with the owners and they'll often tell you about their family's history and talk about life on the farm, turning a tourist experience into a meeting of friends. Some *estancias* offer splendid rooms filled with family antiques. Others are simple affairs where you'll stay in an old farmhouse, and the focus is on peace and quiet. They can be the perfect place to retreat and unwind for a few days or to try an activity such as horse riding or birdwatching. Whichever kind you choose, a good *estancia* will give you an unparalleled taste of traditional hospitality: welcoming strangers is one of the things Argentines do best.

Activities These depend on the *estancia*, but almost all provide horse riding, which is highly recommended even if you've no experience. Galloping across the plains on a *criollo* horse has to be one of the biggest thrills of visiting the country. If you're a beginner, let your hosts know beforehand so that they can arrange for you to ride an especially docile creature. The horse-shy might be offered a ride in a *sulky*, the traditional open horse-drawn carriage, more relaxing but just as much fun. Cattle mustering, meanwhile, may sound daunting but is the best way to get into life on the *campo*. You'll help your hosts move cattle while sitting astride your trusty steed. Gauchos will be on hand to guide you and by the end of the day you'll be whooping and hollering with the best of them.

Prices Usually around US$180/250 per person per night for the most luxurious, to US$65 for the simpler places, but bear in mind that all meals, and often drinks, as well as activities such as horse riding are also included. If this is outside your budget, consider coming for a day visit (*día de campo*), which usually costs around US$60 per person.

Access As *estancias* are inevitably located in the country you'll need to hire a car, although many will pick you up from the nearest town if you don't have one. If you're visiting for a few days ask your hosts to arrange a *remise* taxi; some *estancias* will arrange transfers on request. There are many *estancias* within easy access of Ezeiza International Airport in Buenos Aires, so it can be an ideal way to relax after a long flight at the start of your trip, or to spend your last couple of nights, allowing you to return home feeling refreshed and with vivid memories of Argentine hospitality.

Recommended *estancias* include, **Dos Talas** (pages 98 and 100), **Santa Rita** (page 99), **Juan Gerónimo** (page 99), **Casa de Campo La China** (page 99), **Palantelén** (page), **Ave María** (page 107) and **Siempre Verde** (page 109). A few useful websites are: www.estanciasargentinas.com; www.caminodelgaucho.com.ar and www.raturestancias.com.ar.

with simple but comfortable furniture, a welcoming pool and a long veranda that catches the afternoon sun. Very relaxing.

$$ Bed and Breakfast, Belgrano 39, T02293-426989/1560 7076 (text preferred), hutton@ speedy.com.ar. The most welcoming place in town, charming and helpful English owners. There are 2 comfortable, secluded rooms for couples or families, 1 modern double and the large apartment, **La Torre**, for up to 6, in an idyllic walled garden with small pool. Breakfasts are gorgeous. Host Judy is a delight. Recommended.

$$ Hostal de la Sierra del Tandil, Av Avellaneda 931/41, T02293-422330, www.hostaldeltandil.com.ar. Spanish-style building, with boldly designed rooms with bath, appealing areas to sit, a good restaurant for residents only, and a pool.

$$ Jazmines en la Sierra, Libertad 316, T02293-422873,www.jazminesenlasierra. com.ar. 6 attractive rooms with a colour theme, a lovely cottage garden and slightly less appealing common areas with fireplace.

$$ Plaza de las Carretas, Av Santamarina 728, T02293-447850, www.plazadelascarretas. com.ar. An early 20th-century family house, now a homely and quiet place to stay, with good rooms with eclectic decor and a nice garden at the back.

$$ Hermitage, Av Avellaneda and Rondeau, T02293-423987, www.hermitagetandil.com. ar. Good value in this quiet, old-fashioned hotel next to the park. There are some smart modernized rooms, though these aren't very different to the standard ones, all very simple, but the service is welcoming.

Hostels

$ pp Casa Chango, 25 de Mayo 451, www.casa-chango.com.ar. Bright, colourful hostel set in an old house with lovely communal areas. Central and friendly. Also room for camping.

$ pp Tanta Pacha Hostel, Dabidos 1263, T02293-1554 5967, www.tantapacha.com. Lovely, spacious hostel set in an old country house in attractive grounds. Rustic wooden furniture, dorms only.

Estancias

The real experience of Tandil lies in the beauty of its surroundings, best explored by staying in an *estancia*.

$$$$ Siempre Verde, 45 km southwest of Tandil (next to Barker), T02292-498555, www.estanciasiemprereverde.com. With the most magnificent setting amongst the sierras, this typical 1900s house has a long history. The traditional-style rooms with wonderful old-fashioned bathrooms and lots of antiques have good views over the grounds. The owners, descendants of one of Argentina's most important families, are very hospitable and helpful. Staying here provides a real insight into traditional *estancia* life. Extensive horse riding and walking among the magical sierras in the estate, fishing and *asados* on the hill side. Also offers camping. Highly recommended.

⊘ Eating

Tandil *p105*

Local produce here traditionally includes cheese and sausages, both excellent and served as part of the *picadas* (nibbles with drinks) offered in local bars and restaurants, or available to take away in several good delis in town, such as **Syquet**, General Rodríguez and Mitre, or **Epoca de Quesos**.

$$ 1905, Av Santamarina and San Martín. A minimalist setting in a charming old house that serves excellent, finely elaborate meals.

† El Molino, Juncal 936. A small, simple place with a little windmill, which specializes in different cuts of meat cooked traditionally *al disco* – in an open pan on the fire.

$ El Viejo Sauce, Av Don Bosco and Suiza. Next to the Reserva Sierra del Tigre, in attractive natural surroundings, this is an ideal stopover at tea time for its cakes and home-made jams.

$ Epoca de Quesos, San Martín and 14 de Julio, T02293-448750. An atmospheric 1860s house serving delicious local produce, wines, home-brewed beers and memorable *picadas* to share, which include a great range of cheeses, salami, sausages and traditional pampas bread. Recommended.

$ Parador del Sol, Zarini s/n, T02293-435 697. Located in the attractive *balneario* by Lago del Fuerte, serving great pastas and salads in a smart beach-style trattoria.

$ Taberna Pizuela, Paz and Pinto. Attractive old place serving a broad range of very good simple dishes, including pizzas, their speciality.

🍷 Bars and clubs

Tandil *p105*

Antares, 9 de Julio 758. A popular brewpub, lively in the late evening with excellent beers, good meals and live music every Mon.

Liverpool, 9 de Julio and San Martín. Pictures of the Beatles in this relaxed and friendly bar.

O'Hara, Alem 665. An unbeatable selection of whiskies attracts a mixed crowd. Wines, *tapas* and live music too in this Irish pub.

⛰ Activities and tours

Sierra de la Ventana *p105*

Geotur, San Martín 193, Sierra de la Ventana, T0291-491 5355, www.com-tur.com.ar/ geotur. Trekking, mountain-biking and horse-riding excursions. Also operate a minibus which leaves a few times a day along R76 from Sierra de la Ventana to Tornquist, dropping you off at the entrance to the park.

Tandil *p105*
Golf

Tandil Golf Club, Av Fleming s/n, T02293-406976, www.tandilgolfclub.com.

Horse riding

Gabriel Barletta, Avellaneda 673, T02293-427725. Recommended rides with Gabriel,

expert on native flora, who might end your tour with an informal acoustic guitar session.

Trekking

To find an approved guide who will take you to otherwise inaccessible land for trekking, see www.guiasdetandil.com.ar.

Eco de las Sierras, Maipú 714, T02293-442 741, www.ecodelasierras.com. Run by Lucrecia Ballesteros, a highly recommended guide who is young, friendly and knowledgeable. Day trips (paragliding, lunch and swimming) from US$46,

Kumbre, Av Alvear 124, T02293-434313, www.kumbre.com. Trekking, mountain biking and some climbing guided by experienced Carlos Centineo.

Valle del Picapedrero, T02293-430463, www.valledelpicapedrero.com.ar. Guided walks along a beautiful nearby valley with Ana Maineri, a geology expert.

⊖ Transport

Parque Provincial Ernesto Tornquist *p104*
Bus

La Estrella/El Cóndor has daily services connecting Tornquist and Sierra de la Ventana with Buenos Aires and **Bahía Blanca**. To **Bahía Blanca** also Expreso Cabildo and a few minibus companies.

Tandil *p105*
Bus

To **Buenos Aires**, 5-6 hrs, US$24, with **La Estrella/El Cóndor**, Parque and Río Paraná. Río Paraná goes daily also to **Bahía Blanca**, 6 hrs, US$21, and to **Mar del Plata**, 4 hrs, US$10. El Rápido goes to **Mar del Plata**, 3 hrs, US$11.

Taxi
Alas, on the main plaza, T02293-422222. A *remise* taxi company.

Train
To **Buenos Aires**, 1 service a week, US$8.

Contents

Footnotes

Basic Spanish for travellers

Learning Spanish is a useful part of the preparation for a trip to Latin America and no volumes of dictionaries, phrase books or word lists will provide the same enjoyment as being able to communicate directly with the people of the country you are visiting. It is a good idea to make an effort to grasp the basics before you go. As you travel you will pick up more of the language and the more you know, the more you will benefit from your stay.

General pronunciation

Whether you have been taught the 'Castilian' pronounciation (*z* and *c* followed by *i* or *e* are pronounced as the *th* in think) or the 'American' pronounciation (they are pronounced as *s*), you will encounter little difficulty in understanding either. Regional accents and usages vary, but the basic language is essentially the same everywhere. In Argentina, the accent is distinctly different to the rest of Latin America in one crucial area. The letters *ll* in all other Spanish- speaking countries are pronounced like the *y* in yellow, in Argentina they are pronounced similar to the *sh* in she. The letter *y* in Argentina is also pronounced like the *sh* in she, instead of the *ee* in feet. Another change is that Argentines tend to use *vos* instead of *tú*.

Vowels

a	as in English *cat*
e	as in English *best*
i	as the *ee* in English *feet*
o	as in English *shop*
u	as the *oo* in English *food*
ai	as the *i* in English *ride*
ei	as *ey* in English *they*
oi	as *oy* in English *toy*

Consonants

Most consonants can be pronounced more or less as they are in English. The exceptions are:

g	before *e* or *i* is the same as *j*
h	is always silent (except in *ch* as in *chair*)
j	as the *ch* in Scottish *loch*
ll	as the *y* in *yellow*
ñ	as the *ni* in English *onion*
rr	trilled much more than in English
x	depending on its location, pronounced *x*, *s*, *sh* or *j*

Spanish words and phrases

Greetings, courtesies

hello	*hola*	I speak Spanish	*hablo español*
good morning	*buenos días*	I don't speak Spanish	*no hablo español*
good afternoon/		do you speak English?	*¿habla inglés?*
evening/night	*buenas tardes/noches*	I don't understand	*no entiendo/ no comprendo*
goodbye	*adiós/chao*	please speak slowly	*hable despacio por favor*
pleased to meet you	*mucho gusto*		
see you later	*hasta luego*	I am very sorry	*lo siento mucho/ disculpe*
how are you?	*¿cómo está? ¿cómo estás?*	what do you want?	*¿qué quiere? ¿qué quieres?*
I'm fine, thanks	*estoy muy bien, gracias*	I want	*quiero*
I'm called...	*me llamo...*	I don't want it	*no lo quiero*
what is your name?	*¿cómo se llama? ¿cómo te llamas?*	leave me alone	*déjeme en paz/ no me moleste*
yes/no	*sí/no*		
please	*por favor*		
thank you (very much)	*(muchas) gracias*	good/bad	*bueno/malo*

Questions and requests

Have you got a room for two people?
¿Tiene una habitación para dos personas?
How do I get to_? *¿Cómo llego a_?*
How much does it cost?
¿Cuánto cuesta? ¿cuánto es?
I'd like to make a long-distance phone call
Quisiera hacer una llamada de larga distancia
Is service included?*¿Está incluido el servicio?*
Is tax included? *¿Están incluidos los impuestos?*

When does the bus leave (arrive)?
¿A qué hora sale (llega) el autobús?
When? *¿cuándo?*
Where is_? *¿dónde está_?*
Where can I buy tickets?
¿Dónde puedo comprar boletos?
Where is the nearest petrol station?
¿Dónde está la gasolinera más cercana?
Why?*¿por qué?*

Basics

bank	*el banco*	market	*el mercado*
bathroom/toilet	*el baño*	note/coin	*le billete/la moneda*
bill	*la factura/la cuenta*	police (policeman)	*la policía (el policía)*
cash	*el efectivo*	post office	*el correo*
cheap	*barato/a*	public telephone	*el teléfono público*
credit card	*la tarjeta de crédito*	supermarket	*el supermercado*
exchange house	*la casa de cambio*	ticket office	*la taquilla*
exchange rate	*el tipo de cambio*	traveller's cheques	*los cheques de viajero/ los travelers*
expensive	*caro/a*		

Getting around

aeroplane	*el avión*	insured person	*el/la asegurado/a*
airport	*el aeropuerto*	to insure yourself against	*asegurarse contra*
arrival/departure	*la llegada/salida*	luggage	*el equipaje*
avenue	*la avenida*	motorway, freeway	*el autopista/la*
block	*la cuadra*		*carretera*
border	*la frontera*	north, south, west, east	*norte, sur, oeste*
bus station	*la terminal de*		*(occidente), este*
	autobuses/camiones		*(oriente)*
bus	*el bus/el autobús/*	oil	*el aceite*
	el camión	to park	*estacionarse*
collective/		passport	*el pasaporte*
fixed-route taxi	*el colectivo*	petrol/gasoline	*la gasolina*
corner	*la esquina*	puncture	*el pinchazo/*
customs	*la aduana*		*la ponchadura*
first/second class	*primera/segunda clase*	street	*la calle*
left/right	*izquierda/derecha*	that way	*por allí/por allá*
ticket	*el boleto*	this way	*por aquí/por acá*
empty/full	*vacío/lleno*	tourist card/visa	*la tarjeta de turista*
highway, main road	*la carretera*	tyre	*la llanta*
immigration	*la inmigración*	unleaded	*sin plomo*
insurance	*el seguro*	to walk	*caminar/andar*

Accommodation

air conditioning	*el aire acondicionado*	power cut	*el apagón/corte*
all-inclusive	*todo incluido*	restaurant	*el restaurante*
bathroom, private	*el baño privado*	room/bedroom	*el cuarto/la habitación*
bed, double/single	*la cama matrimonial/*	sheets	*las sábanas*
	sencilla	shower	*la ducha/regadera*
blankets	*las cobijas/mantas*	soap	*el jabón*
to clean	*limpiar*	toilet	*el sanitario/excusado*
dining room	*el comedor*	toilet paper	*el papel higiénico*
guesthouse	*la casa de huéspedes*	towels, clean/dirty	*las toallas limpias/*
hotel	*el hotel*		*sucias*
noisy	*ruidoso*	water, hot/cold	*el agua caliente/fría*
pillows	*las almohadas*		

Health

aspirin	*la aspirina*	contraceptive pill	*la píldora anti-*
blood	*la sangre*		*conceptiva*
chemist	*la farmacia*	diarrhoea	*la diarrea*
condoms	*los preservativos,*	doctor	*el médico*
	los condones	fever/sweat	*la fiebre/el sudor*
contact lenses	*los lentes de contacto*	pain	*el dolor*
contraceptives	*los anticonceptivos*	head	*la cabeza*

| period/sanitary towels | la regla/ las toallas femeninas | stomach | el estómago |
| | | altitude sickness | el soroche |

Family

family	la familia	boyfriend/girlfriend	el novio/la novia
brother/sister	el hermano/la hermana	friend	el amigo/la amiga
daughter/son	la hija/el hijo	married	casado/a
father/mother	el padre/la madre	single/unmarried	soltero/a
husband/wife	el esposo (marido)/ la esposa		

Months, days and time

January	enero	Friday	viernes
February	febrero	Saturday	sábado
March	marzo	Sunday	domingo
April	abril		
May	mayo	at one o'clock	a la una
June	junio	at half past two	a las dos y media
July	julio	at a quarter to three	a cuarto para las tres/ a las tres menos quince
August	agosto		
September	septiembre	it's one o'clock	es la una
October	octubre	it's seven o'clock	son las siete
November	noviembre	it's six twenty	son las seis y veinte
December	diciembre	it's five to nine	son las nueve menos cinco
Monday	lunes		
Tuesday	martes	in ten minutes	en diez minutos
Wednesday	miércoles	five hours	cinco horas
Thursday	jueves	does it take long?	¿tarda mucho?

Numbers

one	uno/una	sixteen	dieciséis
two	dos	seventeen	diecisiete
three	tres	eighteen	dieciocho
four	cuatro	nineteen	diecinueve
five	cinco	twenty	veinte
six	seis	twenty-one	veintiuno
seven	siete	thirty	treinta
eight	ocho	forty	cuarenta
nine	nueve	fifty	cincuenta
ten	diez	sixty	sesenta
eleven	once	seventy	setenta
twelve	doce	eighty	ochenta
thirteen	trece	ninety	noventa
fourteen	catorce	hundred	cien/ciento
fifteen	quince	thousand	mil

Food

avocado	*la palta*	lemon	*el limón*
baked	*al horno*	lobster	*la langosta*
bakery	*la panadería*	lunch	*el almuerzo/la comida*
banana	*la banana*	meal	*la comida*
beans	*los frijoles/*	meat	*la carne*
	las habichuelas	minced meat	*la carne picada*
beef	*la carne de res*	onion	*la cebolla*
beef steak	*el lomo*	orange	*la naranja*
boiled rice	*el arroz blanco*	pepper	*el pimiento*
bread	*el pan*	pasty, turnover	*la empanada/*
breakfast	*el desayuno*		*el pastelito*
butter	*la manteca*	pork	*el cerdo*
cake	*la torta*	potato	*la papa*
chewing gum	*el chicle*	prawns	*los camarones*
chicken	*el pollo*	raw	*crudo*
chilli or green pepper	*el ají/pimiento*	restaurant	*el restaurante*
clear soup, stock	*el caldo*	salad	*la ensalada*
cooked	*cocido*	salt	*la sal*
dining room	*el comedor*	sandwich	*el bocadillo*
egg	*el huevo*	sauce	*la salsa*
fish	*el pescado*	sausage	*la longaniza/el chorizo*
fork	*el tenedor*	scrambled eggs	*los huevos revueltos*
fried	*frito*	seafood	*los mariscos*
garlic	*el ajo*	soup	*la sopa*
goat	*el chivo*	spoon	*la cuchara*
grapefruit	*la toronja/el pomelo*	squash	*la calabaza*
grill	*la parrilla*	squid	*los calamares*
grilled/griddled	*a la plancha*	supper	*la cena*
guava	*la guayaba*	sweet	*dulce*
ham	*el jamón*	to eat	*comer*
hamburger	*la hamburguesa*	toasted	*tostado*
hot, spicy	*picante*	turkey	*el pavo*
ice cream	*el helado*	vegetables	*los legumbres/vegetales*
jam	*la mermelada*	without meat	*sin carne*
knife	*el cuchillo*	yam	*el camote*

Drink

beer	*la cerveza*	cup	*la taza*
boiled	*hervido/a*	drink	*la bebida*
bottled	*en botella*	drunk	*borracho/a*
camomile tea	*la manzanilla*	firewater	*el aguardiente*
canned	*en lata*	fruit milkshake	*el batido/licuado*
coffee	*el café*	glass	*el vaso*
coffee, white	*el café con leche*	hot	*caliente*
cold	*frío*	ice/without ice	*el hielo/sin hielo*

juice	*el jugo*	tea	*el té*
lemonade	*la limonada*	to drink	*beber/tomar*
milk	*la leche*	water	*el agua*
mint	*la menta*	water, carbonated	*el agua mineral con gas*
rum	*el ron*	water, still mineral	*el agua mineral sin gas*
soft drink	*el refresco*	wine, red	*el vino tinto*
sugar	*el azúcar*	wine, white	*el vino blanco*

Key verbs

to go	**ir**
I go	*voy*
you go (familiar)	*vas*
he, she, it goes,	
you (formal) go	*va*
we go	*vamos*
they, you (plural) go	*van*
to have (possess)	**tener**
I have	*tengo*
you (familiar) have	*tienes*
he, she, it,	
you (formal) have	*tiene*
we have	*tenemos*
they, you (plural) have	*tienen*
there is/are	*hay*
there isn't/aren't	*no hay*

to be	**ser** (permanent state) **estar**	
(positional or temporary state)		
I am	*soy*	*estoy*
you are	*eres*	*estás*
he, she, it is,		
you (formal) are	*es*	*está*
we are	*somos*	*estamos*
they, you (plural) are	*son*	*están*

This section has been assembled on the basis of glossaries compiled by André de Mendonça and David Gilmour of South American Experience, London, and the Latin American Travel Advisor, No 9, March 1996.

Menu reader

This is a list of Argentine specialities; for translations of basic food terms, see page 14.

Parrilla and asado

The most important vocabulary is for the various cuts of meat in the *asado*, or barbecue, which you can eat at any *parrilla* or steakhouse.

achuras offal

chinchulines entrails

molleja sweetbread

chorizos beef sausages

morcilla blood sausage

tira de asado ribs

bife ancho entrecôte steak

bife angosto sirloin

bife de chorizo or cuadril rumpsteak

lomo fillet steak

chivito kid

cerdo pork

costilla pork chop

cordero lamb

riñon kidney

pollo chicken

cocina criolla typical Argentine food

empanadas small pasties, traditionally meat, but often made with cheese or other fillings

humitas a puree of sweetcorn, onions and cheese, wrapped in corn cob husks, steamed

tamales corn-flour balls with meat and onion, wrapped in corn cob husks and boiled

locro stew made with corn, onions, beans, and various cuts of meat, chicken or sausage

ciervo venison

jabalí wild boar

bife a caballo steak with a fried egg on top

guiso meat and vegetable stew

matambre stuffed flank steak with vegetables and hard-boiled eggs

horipán hot dog, made with meat sausage

lomito sandwich of thin slice of steak in a bread roll, lomito completo comes with tomato, cheese, ham and egg

fiambre cold meats, hams, salami

picada a selection of fiambre, cheeses and olives to accompany a drink

Fish and seafood

cazuela de marisco seafood stew

merluza hake

manduví river fish with pale flesh

pejerrey inland water fish

pacú river fish with firm meaty flesh

surubí a kind of catfish, tender flesh

camarones prawns

cangrejo crab

centolla king crab

Puddings (*postre*), cakes and pastries

dulce de leche the Argentine obsession – a sweet caramel made from boiling milk spread on toast, cakes and inside pastries

budín de pan a gooey dense bread pudding, often with dried fruit

flan crème caramel, an Argentine favourite

helados ice cream, served piled high in tiny cones

media luna croissant (*dulce or salado* – sweet or savoury)

facturas pastries in general, bought by the dozen

tortilla dry crumbly layered breakfast pastry (in northwest)

torta cake (not to be confused with *tarte*: vegetable pie)

Index

Titles available in the Footprint *Focus* range

Latin America	UK RRP	US RRP
Bahia & Salvador	£7.99	$11.95
Buenos Aires & Pampas	£7.99	$11.95
Costa Rica	£8.99	$12.95
Cuzco, La Paz & Lake Titicaca	£8.99	$12.95
El Salvador	£5.99	$8.95
Guadalajara & Pacific Coast	£6.99	$9.95
Guatemala	£8.99	$12.95
Guyana, Guyane & Suriname	£5.99	$8.95
Havana	£6.99	$9.95
Honduras	£7.99	$11.95
Nicaragua	£7.99	$11.95
Paraguay	£5.99	$8.95
Quito & Galápagos Islands	£7.99	$11.95
Recife & Northeast Brazil	£7.99	$11.95
Rio de Janeiro	£8.99	$12.95
São Paulo	£5.99	$8.95
Uruguay	£6.99	$9.95
Venezuela	£8.99	$12.95
Yucatán Peninsula	£6.99	$9.95

Asia	UK RRP	US RRP
Angkor Wat	£5.99	$8.95
Bali & Lombok	£8.99	$12.95
Chennai & Tamil Nadu	£8.99	$12.95
Chiang Mai & Northern Thailand	£7.99	$11.95
Goa	£6.99	$9.95
Hanoi & Northern Vietnam	£8.99	$12.95
Ho Chi Minh City & Mekong Delta	£7.99	$11.95
Java	£7.99	$11.95
Kerala	£7.99	$11.95
Kolkata & West Bengal	£5.99	$8.95
Mumbai & Gujarat	£8.99	$12.95

Africa	UK RRP	US RRP
Beirut	£6.99	$9.95
Damascus	£5.99	$8.95
Durban & KwaZulu Natal	£8.99	$12.95
Fès & Northern Morocco	£8.99	$12.95
Jerusalem	£8.99	$12.95
Johannesburg & Kruger National Park	£7.99	$11.95
Kenya's beaches	£8.99	$12.95
Kilimanjaro & Northern Tanzania	£8.99	$12.95
Zanzibar & Pemba	£7.99	$11.95

Europe	UK RRP	US RRP
Bilbao & Basque Region	£6.99	$9.95
Granada & Sierra Nevada	£6.99	$9.95
Málaga	£5.99	$8.95
Orkney & Shetland Islands	£5.99	$8.95
Skye & Outer Hebrides	£6.99	$9.95

North America	UK RRP	US RRP
Vancouver & Rockies	£8.99	$12.95

Australasia	UK RRP	US RRP
Brisbane & Queensland	£8.99	$12.95
Perth	£7.99	$11.95

For the latest books, e-books and smart phone app releases, and a wealth of travel information, visit us at: www.footprinttravelguides.com.

footprinttravelguides.com

Join us on facebook for the latest travel news, product releases, offers and amazing competitions: www.facebook.com/footprintbooks.